D0925187

James Ensor

FRONTISPIECE:

Detail, *Entry of Christ into Brussels in 1889*. 1888. Oil on canvas, 8′ 5½″ x 14′ 1½″.
Casino Communal, Knokke-le-Zoute, Belgium

James Ensor

By Libby Tannenbaum

THE MUSEUM OF MODERN ART *NEW YORK*

IN COLLABORATION WITH
THE INSTITUTE OF CONTEMPORARY ART BOSTON
THE CLEVELAND MUSEUM OF ART
THE CITY ART MUSEUM OF SAINT LOUIS

Printed in the United States of America

CONTENTS

FOREWORD

The exhibition accompanying this book is the first definitive one of the works of James Ensor to be held in the United States.

On behalf of the Trustees of the four participating museums, The Museum of Modern Art, The Institute of Contemporary Art, Boston, The Cleveland Museum of Art and the City Art Museum of St. Louis, we wish to express our deepest gratitude to the Belgian Government, whose generous assistance has made the exhibition possible.

The Institute of Contemporary Art through its Director, Mr. James S. Plaut, initiated negotiations for the exhibition with representatives of the Belgian Government, museum officials and owners of Ensor's works. It has been fully responsible for all the arrangements incident to bringing the exhibition to America.

Much of the research for this book has been made possible by a travel grant to Miss Libby Tannenbaum by the Belgian American Educational Foundation, to whose officers we offer grateful acknowledgement.

Finally, we wish to thank the following individuals who have been of outstanding assistance in connection with the exhibition: Dr. Paul Fierens, Chief Curator of the Royal Belgian Museums of Fine Arts, Brussels, M. Robert Giron, Director of the Palace of Fine Arts, Brussels, M. Emile Langui, Art Counsellor to the Belgian Ministry of Public Instruction, Dr. Walther Vanbeselaere, Chief Curator of the Royal Museum of Fine Arts, Antwerp, Dr. Jan-Albert Goris, Belgian Commissioner of Information in the United States, M. Marcel Mabille and M. Gustave Van Geluwe.

ANDREW CARNDUFF RITCHIE

Director, Department of Painting and Sculpture

JAMES ENSOR

PREFACE

The Flemish, in the history of painting, are presented as realists. This is a fact, and more than that, a critical dogma. Let us admit it as the rule; but there are numerous and prodigious exceptions: Bosch, Breugel, Ensor, who are irrealists or surrealists but never, it should be stressed, anti-realists.

The fantasy of the Flemish, or if one prefers, their expressionism, is not in opposition to their inspiration which is naturalistic in the first place, as the eye brings it to the mind. Their imagination feeds upon observation of the concrete, the palpable, the visible, and goes beyond all that. None of the three mentioned above, Bosch, Breugel, James Ensor, prefers idea to object, concept to form and color, symbol to thing symbolized. They are ocular, eye-witnessing men, rather than intellectuals. The exterior world exists powerfully for them. It is by means of elements extracted from nature that their dreams and nightmares are materialized.

Borrowing certain elements from reality, constructing with them mechanisms beyond the control of the reasoning intellect, organisms contrary to logic and marginal to biology—this is the creative process of the masters of drollness, poets of the incongruous, the clownish, the freakish, among whose direct descendants we find the portrayer of the *Entry of Christ into Brussels.*

His point of departure was the real, the earthly, the everyday. But little by little he withdrew his art from the concrete, liberated it from materialism. He never carried it to the point of abstraction but soon ventured into the gratuitously poetic, the phantasmagoric. Gradually his imagination supplanted his observation. Upon the impressionism of his youth he grafted elements of unreality.

The greatest of modern Belgian painters, in his compatriots' opinion—how happy we are to have America also pay tribute to him!—the individual pattern of the evolution of his art is that of post-impressionist painting in general. In some aspects of modernism he has been a follower, in others a forerunner. The work of his young manhood was the result of nineteenth-century tendencies. His mature production, distinctly imbued with expressionism, will serve as a preface or prologue to the history of twentieth-century art.

James Ensor never adhered to any school nor depended upon any specified esthetic. Everything came to him from within himself, even capriciously. But he was not exempt from the influences of his day and age—no artist ever can be—and certainly the derivation from impressionism is as manifest in his case as in Cézanne's, Gauguin's, van Gogh's. He was heretical just as they were. Let us not forget the date of his birth, 1860; four years before that of Toulouse-Lautrec, only four months after Seurat. His early masterworks, the canvases of the so-called "somber" period, from 1879 to 1882, antedate van Gogh's first fumbling efforts and Gauguin's first successes.

And when he died in 1949 he had not ceased to seem modern. The artists of the younger generation, indifferent to most of his contemporaries, still accorded him their sympathy and respect; and gave him credit for starting them off in their several audacious directions.

The course of his lifetime spanned the two centuries which, as we see more and more clearly, contradict and complement one another. The nineteenth century believed in the corporal and the sensory; and its pictorial art was all inclined to the representation of what met the eye. But the twentieth century proposed once more the great question of the spirit. There arose artists of pure intellect (with whom, of course, Ensor had no affinity). There arose artists of free imagination, poet-painters. A good while before the turn of the century, the crossroads, the deviating point, Ensor was the prophet of the unrealistic lyricism of today.

Certain notable works of the beginning of his career, such as *The Lamp Boy* and *The Somber Lady,* revolutionary, it seems, in terms of nineteenth-century esthetics, now stand simply in the ancient tradition of the Flemish old masters, realists and virtuosi, with a subject matter of the common people or the middle classes, a somewhat painstaking truthfulness, and a thick and handsome application of paint. But in later years he led us into another world, having nothing to do with any ordinary walk of life; a world in his own image, mischievous and exorbitant.

As we follow the metamorphoses of his spirit through the years, in the chronology of his canvases, his drawings, and his etchings, finally he seems to require of us a change of our eyeglasses if not of our eyes. The logic of life gives way to dreams. We lose our footing in reality; we are swept up into heavenly fantasy and fairyland. Finally Ensor ceases even to think in the sense of prose. Away his imagination flies whenever it pleases, as though to take part in Watteau's *fêtes galantes,* in Rowlandson's wild satires, in Turner's dream world.

On the one hand Caliban, on the other hand Ariel! In the case of Ensor we need not choose; the one never entirely predominates over the other. Both are in his nature, and the duality endears him to us and adds to our admiration. He is the all-around artist, master of the seen and the unseen, of mind and of matter.

PAUL FIERENS
Chief Curator of the
Royal Belgian Museums of Fine Arts

Translated by Monroe Wheeler

OPPOSITE: *Woman Eating Oysters.* 1882. Oil on canvas, 81⅜ x 59". Royal Museum of Fine Arts, Antwerp

ENSOR

OPPOSITE: *Scandalized Masks*. 1883. Oil on canvas, 53 x 44".
Royal Museum of Fine Arts, Brussels

BELOW: *Carnival on the Beach*. 1887. Oil on canvas, 21⅝ x 25½″.
Collection Mme Van Weyenbergh, Quaregnon, Belgium

ENSOR

BELOW: *Attributes of the Studio*. 1889. Oil on canvas, 32½ x 44½".
Collection Roland Leten, Ghent

BELOW: *Skeletons Fighting for the Body of a Hanged Man*. 1891.
Oil on canvas, 23¼ x 29⅛". Royal Museum of Fine Arts, Antwerp

CiVET.
ENSOR

BELOW: *Intrigue*. 1890. Oil on canvas, 35½ x 59″.
Royal Museum of Fine Arts, Antwerp

BELOW: *The Skate*. 1892. Oil on canvas, 31½ x 39¼".
Royal Museum of Fine Arts, Brussels

ACKNOWLEDGMENTS

This study took its first form in a master's thesis presented at the Institute of Fine Arts, New York University, in 1942. In its preparation I was guided and helped by Professor Walter W. S. Cook, Dr. Robert Goldwater, Professor Richard Offner, Mr. Carl O. Schniewind, Mr. James Johnson Sweeney, Mr. Constant Van der Wall, and by Dr. Jan-Albert Goris, Belgian Commissioner of Information in the United States, who has been a continuing source of counsel and aid.

The Belgian American Educational Foundation made possible my research in Belgium in 1946-47 and 1950, and I wish to thank Mr. Perrin C. Galpin, Mr. E. Clark Stillman and Mr. Jacques Van der Belen, officers of the Foundation, for their kind interest.

In Belgium it was my particular privilege to know the late Mademoiselle Augusta Boogaerts, a close friend of Ensor since his early years. I was made to feel warmly welcome to share her home with its splendid collection, her books, letters, photographs, and with a characteristic generosity and enthusiasm, she supplied invaluable information about the artist and his works.

M. Georges Willems, of Brussels, who is preparing a catalogue raisonné of Ensor's works, was also especially generous with important advice and help.

Photographs were obtained through the courtesy of M. Paul Coremans of the Photographic Archives at the Musée du Cinquantenaire, Brussels, and also from M. Willems. Many others have graciously helped me in the long course of this study. Besides the collectors named here in the list of Lenders to the Exhibition, I wish particularly to thank Mademoiselle Julienne Boogaerts, Mr. C. S. Collinson, Madame Richard Daveluy, M. Paul Fierens, Madame Charles Franck, M. Robert Giron, MM. Luc and Paul Haesaerts, M. Louis Lebeer, M. Marcel Mabille, M. Henry van de Velde, M. Auguste Van Yper.

Mr. Alfred H. Barr, Jr., Mr. Andrew Carnduff Ritchie and Mr. Monroe Wheeler read and corrected the manuscript and have been importantly helpful in other ways, and I am sincerely grateful to them, to Miss Frances Pernas and Mr. Edward L. Mills who so skillfully transformed the manuscript into a book, and to the many members of the Museum of Modern Art staff who have been generous with assistance.

L.T.

CHRONOLOGY

1860 James Sydney Ensor born Ostend, Belgium, April 13. The son of James Frederic Ensor, an Englishman, and Maria Haegheman, daughter of an Ostend family

1877–80 Studied at the Brussels Academy, under Portaels and others

1880 Return to Ostend

1881 Exhibited with *L'Essor* and other groups, and at Brussels Salon

1882 Two paintings exhibited at Paris Salon

1884 All Ensor's entries rejected by Brussels Salon. Formation of exhibiting group *Les XX*

1886 First etchings

1887 Death of the artist's father

1889 *The Entry of Christ into Brussels* refused by *Les XX*, and there was a vote for Ensor's expulsion from the group. This painting was not exhibited until the Brussels retrospective of 1929

1892 The first monograph on Ensor, by Eugène Demolder

1896 One-man show in Brussels, organized by Demolder. *The Lamp Boy* acquired by the Brussels Museum

1898 Ensor exhibition in Paris under the auspices of the French review *La Plume*, with special numbers of the magazine reproducing a large selection of his work

1903 Ensor created a Chevalier of the Order of Leopold

1908 Monograph by the Belgian poet Emile Verhaeren

1913 First catalogue of Ensor's prints published by Garvens-Garvensburg in Hanover, Germany

1914–18 World War I and German occupation of Belgium. Ensor remained in Ostend and received many visits from German artists during this period. His mother died in 1915, his aunt in 1916. The artist was now for the first time master in his own household. He continued to run the family souvenir shop

1921 Retrospective exhibition in Antwerp. First collection of his writings published

1927 Large exhibition at Kestner-Gesellschaft in Hanover

1929 Retrospective exhibition of 325 works in Brussels. Ensor created a baron by the Belgian King

1932 179 works shown at Musée National du Jeu de Paume in Paris

1939 Exhibition of 211 works in Paris, under the auspices of the *Gazette des Beaux-Arts*

1939–45 World War II. Ensor again remained in Ostend, which was heavily bombed. *Sick Tramp Warming Himself*, *Haunted Furniture*, a still life, and a complete set of his etchings were lost in the destruction of the Ostend Museum. The artist's house at 27 rue de Flandre lost most of its windows, and he was forced to stay for a time at the Hotel Regina next door

1942 False report of Ensor's death broadcast in Belgium, and circulated throughout the world by the Belgian News Agency in December. Many obituaries and memorial articles published

1946 Large exhibition at the National Gallery in London

1949 November 19, Ensor died after an illness of three weeks. Buried in the cemetery of the small church at Mariakerke after lying in state in the Town Hall of Ostend

1950 26 of his important paintings shown at the Biennale Exhibition in Venice

James Ensor

The sands of the beach are a world of death, the meeting place of the earth's two faces, land and sea — the double death of drowned land-things thrown up by waves, the death of sea-things choked in dryness. Only the beach could have been the birthplace and the dwelling place of such an artist as James Ensor, who was born in Ostend on the Belgian coast of the North Sea in the spring of 1860. Eighty-nine years later, in November 1949, he died in a shabby house on the rue de Flandre, Belgium's first artist of major importance since Rubens. The rue de Flandre, whose small houses with street-floor shops end at the sea a block away, had hardly changed. Ensor had clung to it for almost a century, through two great wars and an international fame that led to his being named a baron by the Belgian King in 1929.

Belgium is a small country with a proud painting tradition. A national figure, the artist was carried to his grave with official pomp, and if the rue de Flandre had hardly changed, the great funeral cortège drew slowly through an Ostend which had been bombed to a shambles in the 1940's. The bombs had passed over the head of a very old man with a white beard, who had walked on the beach with death for a long time. Death had at last caught up with him, but appropriately it was not death from without, the world disaster, the catastrophic event. It was rather, after nine stubborn decades, the death that is the condition of human

Dunes. 1876. Oil on cardboard, 7 x 9″. Collection Mlle Julienne Boogaerts, Brussels

Estaminet. 1877. Oil on cardboard, 7½ x 9¼″. Gustave Van Geluwe, Brussels

Mystic Death of a Theologian. 1880. Drawing, 47¼ x 41¼″. Collection Marcel Mabille, Brussels

existence, the natural death, the death of decay. "Our bodies begin to fail from our twentieth year . . . we are fated to descend and not to rise—but genius will save us."[1]

A member of the powerful generation that included such artists as van Gogh, Seurat, Lautrec, Ensor had done his most important work before 1900. Unlike the others, he had lived on to become, as it were, his own heir. Lived on like George Bernard Shaw, another stalwart of that generation whom he in some ways resembles, to a clownish senility. A self-portrait of 1938, a deliberate and keenly pointed farce which has its own mocking genius, wears the inscription: "This portrait like its author, is in a state of decay." The young painter of half a century before would have wanted no more from himself than this discomforting

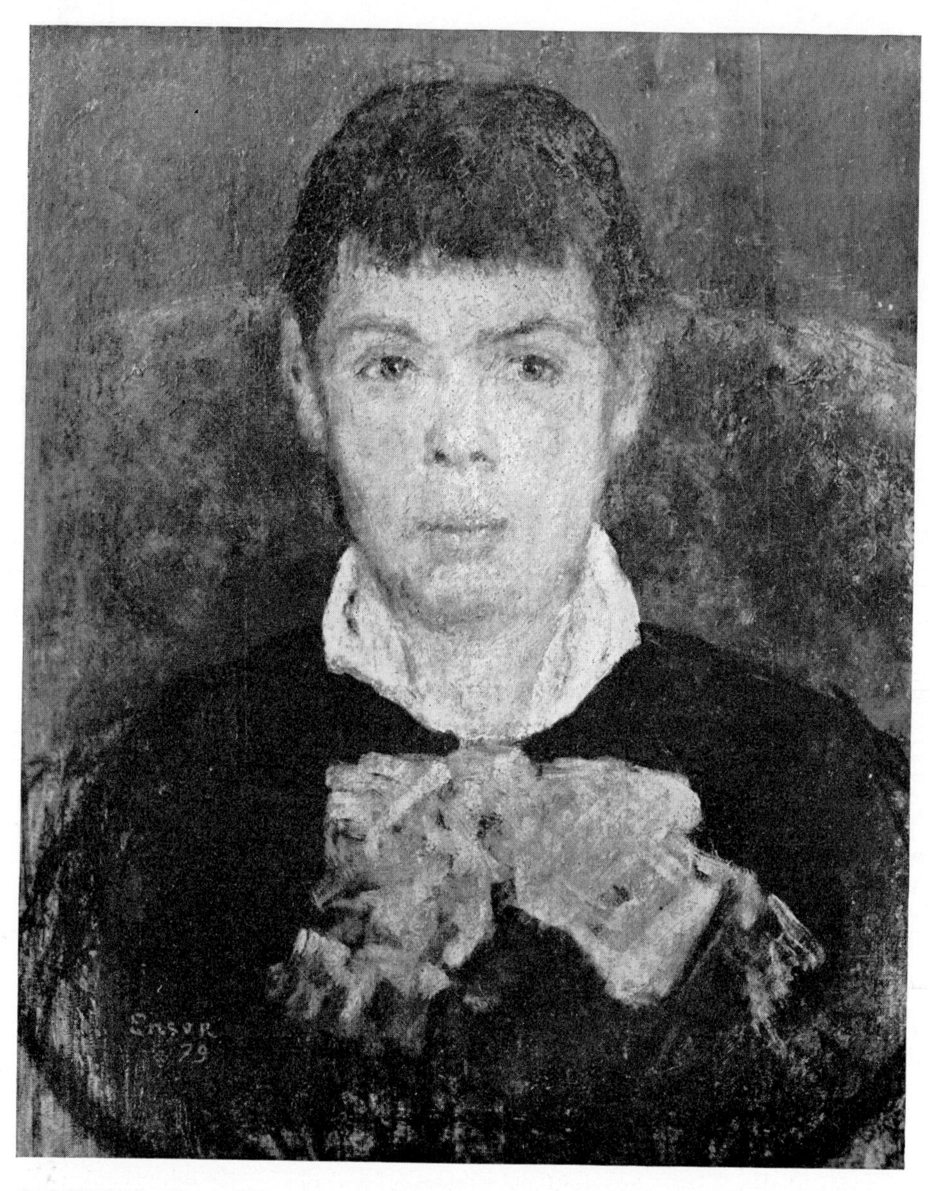

Girl With the Turned-Up Nose. 1879. Oil on canvas, 21¼ x 17¾″. Royal Museum of Fine Arts, Antwerp

truth. Vividly, in the paint of his canvases and the ink of his prints, he had contributed to the record of human consciousness and sensibility, projected his own intense vision into another order of duration and extension — "to speak to the men of tomorrow."[2] James Ensor, baron, "prince of painters," went to his grave after long years of honors with a singing confidence that he had, out of his genius and with his own hands, made his immortality.

PREPARATION: THE EARLY YEARS

The poet Verhaeren in his 1908 monograph describes the child Ensor playing on the beach with the seashells whose nacreous mysteries were to continue to fascinate him. Wind-bitten Ostend, with its channel steamers and its fishing fleet, was also in the 1860's a popular international "watering place" for six hectic weeks each summer. The Flemish family of Ensor's mother kept a souvenir shop on the ground floor of the house on the rue de Flandre. Sea shells, fans, porcelain, chinoiseries, puppets, and carnival masks — much of the "furniture" of Ensor's paintings. His formal schooling extended over only two years, and James Ensor's real education was probably in large part directed by his father, an expatriate Englishman who had been trained in Continental universities. Illustrated books delighted the boy and he loved to copy the pictures in color. It has been noted that Madame Ensor encouraged her son in the hope that he might produce "hand-painted" pictures to be sold in the shop. He was given lessons by two obscure local watercolorists, and painted the countryside around Ostend, the dune-swept beach

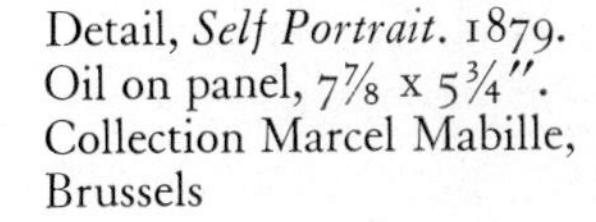

Detail, *Self Portrait.* 1879.
Oil on panel, 7⅞ x 5¾".
Collection Marcel Mabille,
Brussels

Young Sailor. 1880.
Charcoal drawing, 28¾ x 23¼″.
Collection Mlle Julienne Boogaerts, Brussels

and the sea. The small paintings which date from 1876 when Ensor was sixteen years old have an extraordinary rain-washed freshness of vision and color, and Louis Dubois, "the Belgian Courbet," seeing the work of the boy while on a visit to Ostend, encouraged and assisted the young artist.

In 1877 Ensor entered the Brussels Academy. He was later to record the contradictory teachings of the various masters in the amusing playlet *Three Weeks at the Academy*.

> Moral: The student quits the Academy and becomes a *Vingtiste*.*
> Further moral: The *Salon* rejects his paintings.

Ensor, however, remained at the Academy not for three weeks but for three years. Ironically, perhaps, his only distinction was a second prize for drawing from the antique. But, like Gustave Moreau, the director Portaels, though an insignificant painter, was a teacher of the first order. Impressed with his young pupil's force and originality, Portaels kept Ensor's school study *Mystic Death of a*

**Les XX*, which held the first of its annual exhibitions in Brussels in 1884, was the most notable of the many exhibiting art societies in Belgium in the late nineteenth century. It was created out of the dissatisfaction of the more progressive artists with the policies of *L'Essor*, an earlier group, and took its name from its founding directorate of twenty painters and sculptors. Ensor was among the first *Vingtistes*. In the years until 1894, when the artists ceded the directorship to Octave Maus and the group became *La Libre Esthétique*, *Les XX* exhibitions showed a uniquely courageous and discerning selection not only of Belgian art, but of contemporary art from other countries. See bibl. no. 50

The Lamp Boy. 1880. Oil on canvas, 59¾ x 35¾″. Royal Museum of Fine Arts, Brussels

Still Life. 1880. Oil on canvas, 31½ x 39¼″. Museum of Fine Arts, Tournai, Belgium

Theologian (page 29) in his personal collection until he died. The Academy assignments ran to the grand manner, and in Ensor's complete title for this drawing, *Exalted Monks Reclaiming the Body of the Theologian Sus-Oris Despite the Opposition of the Bishop F(T)riton or F(T)riston,* his prankish humor is already apparent.

Ensor's more personal works of 1879, the self portraits and the canvas *Girl with the Turned-Up Nose* (page 30) now in the Antwerp Museum, have by contrast a direct and sure simplicity of statement and a fullness of character amazing as the productions of a nineteen-year-old art student. Ensor is a phenomenon of gifted precocity in the history of art. On his return to Ostend in 1880, he brought with him a developed technical mastery which was immediately to show itself in

Boulevard Van Iseghem at Ostend. 1881.
Oil on panel, 13 x 10¼″.
Collection Mlle Julienne Boogaerts, Brussels

completely mature works, and an intense preoccupation with the representation of the human figure and the problems of figure composition.

On the one hand, he found ready models in the local fishermen and servant types, and in the many charcoal drawings of this year the rough garments and wind-bitten features of these folk are almost carved into broad, angular planes. Unsentimental and severe, these drawings nonetheless express an unaffected natural sympathy and remarkable sensitivity to the particular character of the model. With *The Lamp Boy* (page 33) the substance of these studies is carried onto canvas. Many critics have noted the obvious suggestion of Manet in the subject and the bold silhouetting of the dark figure against the light background. Actually Ensor here is perhaps closer to the environment and tradition of Frans Hals, from whose paintings in the museums Manet derived this type of composition. In any case, this was the first of Ensor's canvases to win official recognition in Belgium. It was acquired by the Brussels Museum in 1896, sixteen years after it was painted.

Most of the early work, however, is made up of portraits of the Ensor family

Lady with a Fan. 1880. Oil on canvas, 52⅛ x 33″. Collection J. Janssen, Antwerp

and friends, with the attempt to set these figures into their home environment of the middle-class, domestic interior. Intimate — and often sentimental — scenes of people reading, listening to music, women sewing or toying with their fans, form a genre that was internationally popular in the middle years of the nineteenth century, and continued to dominate the compositions of such artists as Bonnard and Vuillard in the twentieth. Ensor's early paintings in this genre are distinguished for their calm dignity and the subtlety of nuance in their lighting and atmosphere. Within its nineteenth-century framework, there is a quietness of mood and a luminosity in such a painting as the *Russian Music* (page 40) of 1881, which remind us that this type of middle-class domestic scene had its more ultimate beginnings in the works of the Dutch Vermeer and de Hooch.

In contrast to French *plein-airisme,* the impressionism of Ensor's interior scenes has the restrained gray light of the north, the careful balance between the warm rose tones and the cool blues enforcing the tranquil effect. A heavy impasto is characteristic for this period during which Ensor often drew with the palette knife, and this contributes to the fullness of atmosphere in all his early paintings, where the air seems to move about the scene in heavy and almost tangible waves. The caution with which Ensor introduced more than one figure into these domestic scenes is significant of his deliberate artistry. He was not for several years yet to attempt a single painting with more than two figures.

The *Lady with a Fan* (opposite) is a posed studio portrait of Ensor's sister. In the oil sketch for the *Bourgeois Salon* (page 38), this formality is relaxed and we see her in the natural setting of the Ensor living room, still holding her fan, standing in front of the table at the lower right, looking out of the picture. In the final version of the *Bourgeois Salon* (page 39), two women, one with her back to the spectator, the other seen in profile, are seated at the table reading and sewing. The spectator is moved back and a large expanse of the room is shown in the characteristically up-tilted perspective of impressionism. The domestic quiet of the scene is distinctively and intimately felt. The peculiar animation of the whole canvas by a sharp breaking of the light on the detailed surfaces of the furniture, the pattern of the rug etc., suggests the influence of the Belgian Henri de Braekeleer. In the painting *Afternoon at Ostend* (page 41) in the Antwerp Museum, this setting is moved up closer to the observer and the little social drama of the afternoon tea introduced. The figures are Ensor's mother with his sister, wearing a bonnet and staring boldly out of the picture, pretending to be the guest.

The very title of the painting *Russian Music* identifies the romanticism which pervades this bourgeois culture. A comparison of this 1881 canvas with the 1883 *Listening to Schumann* of Fernand Khnopff, who had been a fellow student of

Ensor's at the Academy, and was associated with him in *Les XX,* demonstrates at once the appeal this type of composition had for Belgian painters in this period, and the superior integrity and sensitivity Ensor brought to it. Whereas in the Khnopff painting[3] the woman covers her face with her hands in the quasi-intensity of her emotion or concentration, the gentleman of *Russian Music* (who is Ensor's friend, the painter Willy Finch), sits comfortably with his legs crossed and his hands in his lap and enjoys the music. He is identified as a visitor by the silk hat on the table; only the back of the girl who is playing the piano is seen. Far from provincial sentimentality, Ensor's is a quiet cool restraint here that is equalled only by Degas at this time. The economy of accessory and the wholly unified organization of the predominantly horizontal-vertical elements are also characteristic of Ensor's 1881 portrait of his father in the Brussels Museum.

In sharp contrast is the *Portrait of the Artist's Mother* (page 42). Accessories of setting which make the other portraits in this group in a sense typical as repre-

The Bourgeois Salon. 1880. Oil sketch, on canvas, 25⅝ x 22½". Collection Gustave Van Geluwe, Brussels

The Bourgeois Salon. 1881. Oil on canvas, 51⅛ x 43¼". Collection Mme Henri Jooris, Lille, France

Russian Music. 1881.
Oil on canvas, 52⅜ x 43¼″.
Royal Museum of Fine Arts,
Brussels

sentatives of a class, are here completely eliminated in a direct and powerful insistence on the personality of the sitter. The rigid posture of the figure, the tightly folded hands, the harsh composure of the features indicate the peasant obduracy of this woman. The strength and shrewdness which enabled Madame Ensor to hold her family together and indeed to support them all by her management of the family souvenir shop, are likewise apparent. Ensor had learned to "draw with light" and in the ability forcefully to express the personality of his sitter purely by the subtle modeling of the features in an almost abstract chiaroscuro, he here suggests Rembrandt.

Ensor's masterpiece among these early domestic scenes is the large canvas *Woman Eating Oysters* of 1882 (page 11), which expresses a delight in the rich facts of existence that is almost specifically Flemish. The figure is combined with a magnificent still life, and Ensor's pleasure in the delineation of textures is given full rein in bold and joyous brushstrokes: the mirrored sideboard behind the woman, the white napery, the gleam of china and glass on the table, the shining wetness of the oysters themselves — these are radiant in an air which seems to have its own rich substantiality.

In the two years since he had returned from the Academy, Ensor had lightened

Afternoon at Ostend. 1881. Oil on canvas, 42½ x 52⅜". Museum of Fine Arts, Antwerp

Portrait of the Artist's Mother. 1881. Oil on canvas, 39¼ x 31½". Royal Museum of Fine Arts, Brussels

Portrait of the Painter in a Flowered Hat. 1883.
Oil on canvas, $29\frac{1}{2} \times 23\frac{5}{8}''$.
Collection Mlle Julienne Boogaerts, Brussels

and brightened his palette to achieve in this painting a form of post-impressionism closely related to that taken up by Vuillard and Bonnard in Paris a decade later. And now, at the early age of twenty-two, he had the distinction of having gone beyond his contemporaries' comprehension. The uncommon success of the first works in their showings with such exhibiting groups as *La Chrysalide* and *L'Essor,* the approval of the Brussels Salon, and the triumph of the acceptance of the 1880 *Colorist* and *Chinoiseries* by the Paris Salon in 1882, now gave way to a concerted slamming of doors which stupefied the young artist. In 1882 *Woman Eating Oysters* was refused by the Antwerp Salon; in the next year it was refused by the supposedly avant-garde group *L'Essor.* In 1884 his whole contribution, which included also the *Afternoon at Ostend,* was to be refused by the Brussels Salon with the comment, "There will certainly be much worse canvases in the exhibition, but we cannot admit these tendencies." Criticism of his work was to become more and more simply a matter of uncontrolled and outrageous epithet, and Ensor was driven back into isolation in Ostend and complete financial dependence on his mother, who was getting very much more than the "hand-painted pictures" she had bargained for.

In 1929, when Ensor was created a baron by the Belgian King, it was in recognition of precisely these very early pictures which had brought down such a storm half a century before. Their marvelous and subtle color was lauded: the works of the intervening years, which constitute Ensor's more personal and truly significant contribution to the mainstream of modern painting, were ignored or at best minimized by the official critics as the unfortunate result of some extraordinary disease which had enfeebled the artist in his early twenties.

The virulence of the contemporary reaction to Ensor's color innovations was at last significantly to embitter his work itself, but long before the full effects of this could have been felt there are indications that the living room above the souvenir shop knew other scenes besides those of quiet middle-class satisfaction.

The *Somber Lady* (opposite) of 1881 is Ensor's first indication of an alive preoccupation with the starker aspects of human drama and the ability to express this in vivid pictorial terms. The tense silhouette of the darkly-clad figure against the bright light of the window, the jagged zig-zag movement of the lines of the composition itself, are contrived for a highly expressive effect. There is no particular story, and there is nothing heroic or on the grand scale in this little private drama. It is seen in all the domestic intimacy of the other early interior scenes, but a note of tension is sounded.

The *Somber Lady* stands in the same relation to these other middle-class interiors as the 1882 canvas *Sick Tramp Warming Himself* (page 46) does to the earlier *Lamp Boy*. In this painting which was unhappily destroyed in the burning of the Ostend Museum during the last war, Ensor viewed with a trenchant sympathy the sick tramp, the "lousy fellow" with his chair drawn up to the warmth of the small stove, his only comfort and companion in the cracked walls of his house. Realistic scenes of lower-class life had persisted as one of the dominant motives of Flemish painting. In his writings Ensor was to ridicule the "vast metallic lie" of Meunier's heroizations of working men. In what now becomes his own selection of types — poachers, tramps, drunkards — he himself presents figures that are not merely members of the lower classes. They are outcasts from any class and represent Ensor's first insistence on man at his most abject and inglorious. The species had appeared in the pictures of Teniers and Brouwer, but in the objective rendering of the outcast at his most forlorn, Ensor's excursions into this genre are far from the seventeenth-century's good-humored amusement.

In *The Drunkards* (page 47) of the next year, the shabby figure who stares out of the picture from one side has only silent sympathy to offer his companion

Somber Lady. 1881. Oil on canvas, 39¼ x 31⅞″. Royal Museum of Fine Arts, Brussels

whose glass now lies under the table on which he hides his head in his hands. The bottle between them on the center of the table stands out sharply against a poster advertising a farm for sale. Of all Ensor's works, this painting approaches most closely to nineteenth-century moralizing: it is saved by a cruel honesty, the conveyed sense of a whole dreary past.

Sick Tramp Warming Himself. 1882. Oil on canvas, 38⅝ x 34⅝". Formerly in the collection of the Ostend Museum, destroyed during World War II

The Drunkards. 1883. Oil on canvas, 45¼ x 65". Collection Dr. Delporte, Brussels

MASKS AND SKELETONS: 1883-1887

The painting of *The Drunkards* marks the end of Ensor's first period, and as beginnings are often contained in endings, another painting of 1883, the *Scandalized Masks* (page 13) which is in its formal aspects very close to *The Drunkards,* announces new and strange beginnings. For with this painting Ensor first realized the possibilities of the mask which was to become the dominant motive of his work in the years beginning with the great *Entry of Christ into Brussels* in 1888. Ensor's name has become almost synonymous with masks. So completely were they finally to usurp his interest in the human figure itself that in his later years when the painter approached portraiture, his figures are conceived as a reanimation of the mask on a mechanical rather than an organic level in that the figures become puppets.

The source of the masks was the carnival which was most elaborately celebrated

Portrait of the Artist's Aunt. c.1883. Pencil, 8$\frac{1}{4}$ x 6$\frac{1}{4}$″. Mlle Julienne Boogaerts

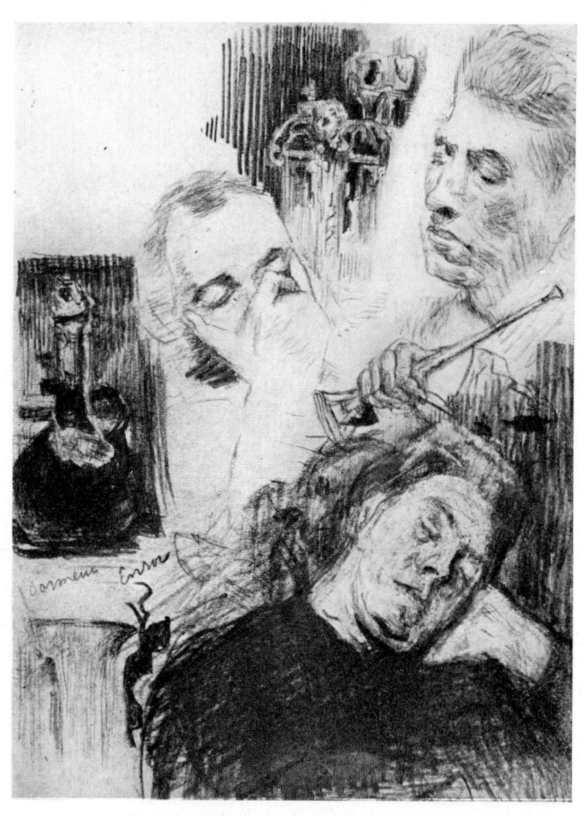

Sleep. c.1883. Pencil sketch, 8$\frac{3}{4}$ x 6$\frac{1}{4}$″. Collection Mlle Julienne Boogaerts, Brussels

in Ostend, where the natives have little work during the long dull winter season. Even today one often sees bands of people in fancy dress parading through the streets of Belgium. Ensor writes that when his grandmother Haegheman was sixty years old she still donned mask and costume for the fête. In *Scandalized Masks* a blue-spectacled shrew enters through the door, clutching a musical horn which she waves menacingly at the stupefied long-nose who has been sitting alone with his half-emptied bottle. The whole scene exists in an aura of some mysteriously intimate evil.

Ensor was twenty-three when he painted *Scandalized Masks.* This same year a large group of his paintings was shown at *L'Essor.* The refusal from the Brussels Salon did not come until the next year, and the achievement of the Paris Salon the year before must still have been a source of pride to the young artist. *Scandalized Masks* was shown at the first exhibition of *Les XX* in 1884, and in her chronicle of the group Madeleine Maus notes: "Strangely enough, this first year its quality

Portrait of the Artist's Mother. c.1883. Pencil, 8¾ x 6¼″. Mlle Julienne Boogaerts, Brussels

intimidated the critics; the attacks came a little later." Thus, while there can be no question but that the intrigues and attacks of his critics were to play a major role in confirming Ensor in an art of resentment and hatred of mankind, the real thrusts had not yet come, and the sense of outrage which pervades so early a work as *Scandalized Masks* must be explained on some other grounds.

Ensor's father, the disinherited son of a cultivated English family, had never become more than an exile in the small bourgeois shopkeeping circle of Ostend into which he had married. He had been trained as an engineer and soon after the marriage came to the United States seeking a position. The Civil War broke out a few months after his arrival and discouraged the elder Ensor who returned to Ostend. And from this episode in 1861 until his death in 1887 he made no further effort to find a place for himself in the world. Ensor described him as a sensitive intellectual, loving classical music, drawing a little, inclined to be distant with people. The menage in Ostend included his wife's mother and unmarried sister, all shrewd, hard, shopkeeping Flemish women, and he found his only escape in the taverns. In 1887 he died in the streets of Ostend of the effects of alcohol and exposure. The unpleasantness of the family life is indicated by Ensor's observation that the scenes in his parents' house and the fear that he might be as unhappy as his father always prevented his own marriage.

The menace of the bottle hauntingly isolated on the table in both paintings now becomes clear. *Scandalized Masks* is no more fantastic than *The Drunkards,* but it wears the carnival masks of Ostend. There are weirdness and mystery in these

Pencil sketch. c.1883. 6¾ x 8¾". Collection Mlle Julienne Boogaerts, Brussels

Figures. c.1880. Watercolor, 9⅝ x 13″. Museum of Fine Arts, Ghent, Belgium

trappings of the carnival, but they are not yet the self-motivated abstractions of humanity to which Ensor was to develop them.

And from 1883 until 1887 Ensor's painting now goes slowly in contrast to the strikingly rich production of his first years. There are, on the other hand, an enormous number of drawings, and beginning in 1886, the etchings. In these, Ensor sounds the extraordinary notes which were to find culmination and fulfillment in the many magnificent paintings of 1888-1892.

The small sketches which he made in cheap copybooks during these years are a miracle of draftsmanship. And they are more. They are heavy with the long dull winter of Ostend, the shop quiet, the whole family — mother, grandmother, sister, aunt, a small cousin who was living with them — all dozing. Only the young artist awake, filling page after page with sketches in which the sleep of the others is woven into haunting compositions that make innovations in the history of art. For he composes each page so that the kaleidoscopic juxtapositions, conventional in any artist's notebook, take on a kind of surrealist unity. The 1883 drawing (page 53) tells a whole story in a bit of carved furniture, a drowsy profile, an ear and a rose. By 1886 the artist superimposes his own brooding image on the great carved chest, as though in that room whose sullen women hibernated in slumber, the restless furniture was by contrast gloomily alive (page 54). The furniture and the artist were equally witnesses in this atmosphere from which Ensor was never to have the resolution to remove himself, and there is a sense of this identification in the way he invests the furniture with his own sense of its horrors.

The important 1885 painting titled *Haunted Furniture* (page 55) was unfortunately among those lost in the destruction of the Ostend Museum. The woman sewing as the little girl sat at the table with her book formed an intimate domestic group in the line of earlier middle-class interiors. But here there was a skeleton at the elbow of the little girl, no longer reading her book, but staring out of the picture, petrified with terror at the hideous and awful presences represented by masks which had insinuated themselves into the bourgeois living room without disturbing the older woman. The great carved chest became a positive and threatening object, the closet of the skeletons. In the earlier domestic scenes the sense of the background as a cube-shaped room is very strong, emphasized by tricks of perspective and the almost invariable introduction of a corner. In *Haunted Furniture* the space is quite shallow, the whole scene set against one wall, the masked specters moving in from both sides as from the wings of a stage. This strict stage-like horizontality becomes very frequent in the later paintings of masks. The inward movement of the menacing figures from both sides of the canvas is extremely effective, suggesting that they must finally converge and swallow up the central scene, which is indeed exactly what happens in many of the later pictures. But the presence of the little girl as protagonist gave *Haunted Furniture* a dramatic clarity which is, in the later pictures, sometimes obfuscated by the lack of any immediately apparent adversary or victim of the masks.

The rich evocative power of *Haunted Furniture* was in no small part due to the completeness with which Ensor here drew upon all his previous studies. The setting of the two figures at a table derives from a whole series of earlier works. The manner in which the little girl stared out of the picture, creating a personal connection which must draw the almost hypnotized observer wholly into the scene is again characteristic, *The Drunkards* providing the immediately preceding example.

But the mask was now dissociated from the carnival to become an abstraction of the frightening and the terrible. Unlike *Scandalized Masks, Haunted Furniture* had become a kind of psychomachia, with the embodiment and representation of elements not actually physically present in the scene. Like all moralists, Ensor sought the allegory, and with society failing to provide any significant pattern which might measure and describe the world, he was thrown back upon his own

Page from notebook. 1883. Pencil, 8¾ x 6⅞″. Private collection, Brooklyn, New York

experience. And here he was particularly fortunate in this deeply personal and at the same time traditional world of the masks which were sold in the family souvenir shop. This world of masks heralds the beginning of the expressionist movement: within it, Ensor is at complete liberty to distort for effect. And yet, intensification and exaggeration of expression being implicit in the very convention of the mask, he avoids the expressionists' need to justify their right to distort. Ensor is able to move swiftly in a direction which was opened to the artists of France and Germany only after a long and arduous tentative period of theorizing. Here in Ostend, he found in the carnival mask the vivid concentration of meaning for which Gauguin was to search in Tahiti and the next generation in African art. The cruelties and absurdities of his personal milieu he was able to project on an abstracted and universal plane which makes him the first of the artists of the *Weltangst* which characterizes so much of late nineteenth- and twentieth-century expression. It is this isolated creation of an art out of the personal and the local that has made Ensor one of the baffling originals. It is his genius for recognizing the elements out of which a new art must be molded that marks his significance as artist-innovator.

Lacking pictorial precedent as it did, Ensor's way was nonetheless in a sense prepared by the very different work of the Belgian Félicien Rops. But where Ensor uses the mask as the true face of evil and stupidity, the "intensified expression," with Rops it performs the exactly reverse function of symbolizing the coquetry which often cloaks actual ugliness and vice. The difference between the essentially metaphysical level on which Ensor is preoccupied with the question of evil as

Self Portrait (Later titled *Mon portrait triste et somptueux*). 1886.
Pencil, 8¾ x 6¼".
Collection Mlle Julienne Boogaerts, Brussels

Haunted Furniture. 1885. Oil on canvas. Formerly in the collection of the Ostend Museum, destroyed during World War II

against the personal fascination it had for Rops is pronounced, and yet the distinction which Rops had made between the outer shell and the inner nature of man was a step which logically precedes the symbolic use of the mask in *Haunted Furniture.*

The mask also figures importantly in the work of Edgar Allan Poe which had become popular in France and Belgium in the translations of Baudelaire. Many of Poe's stories are set in the carnival or the masquerade, and his works are heavy with death, with a weird and brooding atmosphere, with atrocious and secret evil.

The Cruel: Jesus Presented to the People. 1885.
Drawing, 59 x 39¼″.
Collection Marcel Mabille, Brussels

In such a painting as *Haunted Furniture* Poe's unhappy ghosts were made to come to life for the spectator and for the petrified little girl who stared helplessly out of the picture. Ensor's must have been a peculiarly vivid sense of the subtle menace and the cruelties sheathed in the brilliance of Poe's carnival pageant. A drawing of 1880 illustrates *King Pest,* and this appears again among the etchings of 1895. A landscape of 1890 is called *The Domain of Arnheim,* and the prints of *Hop Frog* date from 1898—a devotion to the sympathetic genius of the American over long years. Ensor must have read and reread Poe with a feeling almost of self-discovery.

At this point, Ensor was ready to find in Christian iconography not only a universally accepted protagonist in the Christ, but also a traditional frame for the kind of confrontation of innocence with human vileness and hebetude which he had given an independent pictorial form in *Haunted Furniture*. 1886, the year in which he makes a whole series of drawings of the life of Christ, is also the year in which Ensor's etching begins. There can be no question but that it was this new certainty of the direction of his art, as well as the rich store of sympathetic themes he found ready-made in the Christ cycle, that led the artist to turn now to the reconsideration of technical and formal problems which dominates his work in the next two years.

The etchings are evidence of a reaching out towards a new medium. In the series of drawings of the life of Christ, many of which reappear as prints, Ensor gives the first evidence of a completely new approach towards an intensification of the picture's emotional and evocative impact that anticipates the "esthetic equivalent" of expressionism. Even the titles of these drawings indicate the governing emphasis on mood:

The Gay: The Adoration of the Shepherds
The Cruel: Jesus Presented to the People

Christ Calming the Waters. 1886. Etching, 6⅜ x 9⅜″

Christ in Agony. 1888. Drawing, 23⅜ x 29⅛″. Royal Museum of Fine Arts, Brussels

Calvary. Pencil and color on panel, 6¾ x 8¾″. Mlle Julienne Boogaerts, Brussels

The Ardent and Radiant: The Entry into Jerusalem
The Sad and Broken: Satan and the Fantastic Legions Tormenting the Crucified
The Tranquil and Serene: The Descent from the Cross
The Intense: Christ Ascending into Heaven

It is not the visual but rather the special emotional aspect of his subject that possesses the artist. Ensor was far from the formal emphasis and restraints of his own period: "Pictorially speaking, my technique is allied to the subject"[4] . . . "The artist must invent his style, and each new work demands its own."[5] This was the twentieth-century's "objective correlative."

Both *The Adoration of the Shepherds* and *Jesus Presented to the People* (page 56) suggest Rembrandt in their organization and dramatic lighting. Although much freer, they are in a sense close to the *Mystic Death of a Theologian* (page 29) done at the Academy in 1880, and this tentative looking backward for a precedent is again evidence of Ensor's deliberate artistry. The 1886 etching of *Christ Calming the Waters* (page 57) is a wholly original and strikingly dramatic representation, full of the sense of the power of the small figure in the boat to overcome the tremendous and tempestuous forces of sea and sky. The drawing of the dead Christ watched over by angels (below) is the first of a small group of Ensor's works which is wholly dominated by a kind of symbolic line. The strong, stylized

The Dead Christ Watched Over by Angels. 1886. Drawing, 6¼ x 8½". Collection Marcel Mabille, Brussels

The Cathedral. 1886. Etching, 9½ x 7½″

outlines of the figures which are used here to indicate the vitiated yet strangely clear vision after great emotional and physical strain curiously anticipate the linear *art nouveau* style of the next decade which reappears in many of Ensor's drawings and prints of the 90's.

The drawing *Christ in Agony* (page 58) where the figure on the cross is surrounded by horrible ape-like forms and by skeletons one of which is devouring his flesh, is unique in the history of art; not the Christ of dogma and tradition, but an excrutiatingly tortured and personal vision in which the artist projects himself into the agony of the crucified. That this was indeed the case is evidenced by a later Calvary drawing where the letters at the top of the central cross are not INRI but ENSOR, and the lance piercing the side of the crucified bears a banner on which is written "Fétis," the name of one of Ensor's most virulent critics (page 58).

It is important to remember that it is not with Christ as a divine being but merely as the archetype of persecuted truth that the identification is made. There is nothing of the pious in these drawings. Ensor was always anti-clerical, and indeed, in his later *Scenes From the Life of Christ* approaches farce. Not the Son of God so much as Renan's "exalted man," Ensor's Christ is only a more conscious and deliberate equivalent of the little girl of *Haunted Furniture*. Yet in contrast to the simple-minded gothicizing piety of the works of Maurice Denis and his school, Ensor's religious subjects actually offer a comment on the nature of both men and gods, and in its essence his conception of the Christ at this time is more nearly that which was to be given form by the truly religious Rouault.

Ensor's Christ is symbolic of the attempt to give dignity and meaning to human life mocked and destroyed by the mob. This is one of the artist's most insistent themes. In the 1886 print *The Cathedral* (opposite), the marvellously delineated church stands as a magnificent and sphinx-like monument on which the grotesque members of the carnival mob in the foreground not only turn their backs, but from

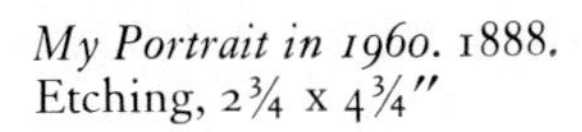

My Portrait in 1960. 1888.
Etching, $2\frac{3}{4} \times 4\frac{3}{4}''$

Iston, Pouffamatus, Cracozie and Transmouff, Celebrated Persian Physicians, Examining the Stools of King Darius after the Battle of Arbela. 1886. Etching, 9⅝ x 7¼″

which they are separated by a packed phalanx of the military. The cathedral is not only a monument to the Savior; it is the work and evidence of human genius, the towering possibility of salvation rising above the greedy mob. One of Ensor's most sincere and thoughtful works, *The Cathedral* is a conception whose significance is immediately felt if not immediately understood in explicit terms, and whose technical mastery in this first year of Ensor's etching has fascinated connoisseurs of the print.

Like the whole series of religious subjects of 1886, *The Cathedral* represents a defiance of human limitations, but in the fantastic works which begin to be frequent in Ensor's work at this time, it is exactly these that he records. The tenderly drawn head of his father in death faces, in the catalogue of Ensor's prints, the gay little skeleton that bears the title *My Portrait in 1960* (page 61). The death of Christ is a symbolic and dramatic event, but the death of a man may be only the end of misery, a triumphant release. From this time until his very latest works, death continues to be Ensor's persistent and characteristic subject. "Our bodies begin to fail from our twentieth year . . . we are fated to descend and not to rise . . ." Disease and death and putrescence are the basic indignity and the inescapable fate. And they are Ensor's weapon against the mob, for it is they, the mockers, who die, and it is genius which is immortal. Sure of his genius, the death of the body delights him. There is often a savage sadism in Ensor's works, a fury against the horrors and absurdities of human existence which did not wait for the invention of "existentialism."

He now begins frequently to be scatological, but here it is important to remember that this is typical of Flemish humor and Mannikinpis is the pride of Brussels. The elaborate mock-Rembrandtesque setting and costumes of the 1886 print, *Iston, Pouffamatus, Cracozie and Transmouff, Celebrated Persian Physicians, Examining the Stools of King Darius after the Battle of Arbela* (opposite), parallels the amusing pomposity of the title. The almost insane concentration of Iston and his colleagues and the intent curiosity of the king are not only a commentary on the constant probing for omens which must amaze the reader of Plutarch; they present such a *reductio ad absurdum* of historical painting in the grand manner as must recall Hogarth, and here indeed, we find the only trace of a similarity in approach

Devils' Sabbath. 1887. Etching, 8⅝ x 10½″

between Ensor and the British artist with whom he is so often compared on the grounds of his father's ancestry.

The humorous extravagance of the title begins to be typical of Ensor. These titles comment on the paintings with the same keenness as those of Paul Klee who was so much influenced by him. Ensor's untranslatable writings are characterized by a gay, uninhibited inventiveness that might be described as a mixture of *Ubu Roi,* James Joyce, and Danny Kaye. "Les suffisances matamoresques appellent la finale crevaison grenouillère."[6]

The print *Devils' Sabbath* (page 63) of 1887 indicates how far Ensor was from the Satanism of such of his contemporaries as Huysmans. The goblins move across the page in a pathetically harum-scarum procession which turns back upon itself in its movement towards a crescent moon. The very frailty of the insect-like shapes is comic.

The contrast between this print and the Museum of Modern Art's painting *The*

JACQUES CALLOT: *Le Pisseur.* Drawing. Uffizi, Florence

Left: *Le Pisseur.* 1887. Etching, 3¾ x 4¼"

The Vengeance of Hop Frog. 1898.
Etching, 14⅜ x 9¾″

Tribulations of Saint Anthony (page 66) of the same year is extraordinary. The demons tormenting the Saint take on fantastic shapes which strongly suggest forms of an older art but which are completely new to Ensor who had not until this time gone beyond masks and skeletons and such animal and insect derived shapes as we find in the *Devils' Sabbath*. The artist who until this time had always kept the number of figures in his paintings down to the barest few now handles a whole galaxy with inexhaustible invention. The formal diagonal composition, the wide panorama behind the group of figures in the foreground, the uninhibited burst of brilliant greens, reds and blues slashed across the canvas, are entirely unlike anything in the artist's work up to this time. *The Tribulations of Saint Anthony* is the

The Tribulations of Saint Anthony. 1887. Oil on canvas, 46⅜ x 66″. The Museum of Modern Art, New York

JACQUES CALLOT: *Temptation of Saint Anthony*. c.1616. Etching

JACQUES CALLOT: *The Temptation of Saint Anthony*. 1635. Etching

one work of Ensor for which those immediately preceding do not constitute a convincing preparation and one is driven to search for some intervening prototype.

Ensor has often been compared with Bosch. The subject here would seem to point to Bosch, but an examination of his work leaves Ensor's *St. Anthony* still unexplained, and rather convinces one of the truth of Ensor's statement that he did not even know Bosch in his early years.

On the other hand it is difficult to understand the complete failure of Ensor's critics to associate him with Jacques Callot, that other great "fantastic" of art his-

Hail Jesus, King of the Jews. 1885. Drawing, 76¾ x 55⅛″. Collection Mme Richard Daveluy, Ostend, Belgium

Detail, *Entry of Christ into Brussels in 1889* (see next page)

tory whose *Gobbi, Balli,* and *Caprices* series show a preoccupation with the mask no less obsessive than Ensor's own. Evidence of a close study of Rembrandt's prints is obvious in Ensor's early etchings, and it was natural that he should turn as well to the bold *commedia dell'arte* of Callot, who first raised etching to the dignity of an independent art. One of Ensor's 1887 etchings, *Le Pisseur,* actually begins as a

Entry of Christ into Brussels in 1889. 1888. Oil on canvas, 8′ 5½″ x 14′ 1½″. Casino Communal, Knokke-le-Zoute, Belgium

replica of a Callot drawing (page 64) which is reproduced in Marius Vachon's study of Callot published in Paris in 1886,[7] and which may have been Ensor's introduction to the artist's works.

The usual reversing occurring in the print, the rough brick work which terminates the wall unmistakably identifies the Callot sketch as the source for Ensor's composition. The scale of the figure is identical, but Ensor gives the gentleman a top hat and makes the plate peculiarly his own by the children's scrawls and the words "Ensor est un fou" which can be read on the wall.

Given this connection *The Tribulations of St. Anthony* becomes comprehensible. Among Callot's works there are two etchings of this subject (page 67). Both have the broad diagonal composition with the foreground frame of figures which appears for the first time in Ensor's painting. Ensor's stream with its mask which floats up out of the water corresponds in the composition to Callot's early print where a boat in the shape of a demon appears in the stream. In Callot's later version the river bed becomes simply a dry ravine, but here we find at the far side the colonnaded buildings which stand across the river in Ensor's work. Ensor moves the Saint himself to the foreground and still tends to create his own demons out of a juxtaposition of shapes from animal or sea life, and it is the crustacean which predominates here. The intervention of Callot in widening his scope and liberating his imagination is, however, marked. The grotesque horseplay which appears here in Ensor's work for the first time takes its motives directly from the Callot prints.

But a balloon appears among the flying figures and the musician wears the uniform of the town band. The bewildered look of Ensor's Saint as he looks up from his book, seeming hardly to understand what is going on, is unique. This painting is one of the clearest representations of the singular lack of personal attraction the conventional temptations had for Ensor. It would, indeed, be difficult to conceive of a St. Anthony more different from Rops'. Ensor's Saint is faced not with "temptation," but, as the title indicates — "tribulations."

Again, as in the case of the Poe illustrations which continue sporadically in Ensor's work until the end of the century, the importance of the influence of Callot on the artist is confirmed by a continuing reference to his compositions. Ensor's 1895 etching, *The Battle of the Golden Spurs* (page 97), certainly owes itself in large measure to the suggestion of Callot's tournament prints. *Fridolin and Gragapança of Yperdam* (page 100), a portrait of the artist and Eugène Demolder on a walking trip through the Low Countries, makes an amusing reference to the *commedia dell'arte* of Callot's *Balli* series. In the various versions of *Hop Frog* (page 65), Ensor brings together with particular genius Callot and Poe, his two progenitors in the study of carnival.[8]

In Jacques Callot, then, Ensor had found, as it were, an artistic parentage. Where the works up to this meeting with Callot's bold and fantastic spirit are in a sense tentative and experimental, as though Ensor were not altogether certain of the validity of his excursions into the expressionist world of the carnival and the grotesque, he now forges ahead in this vein with a sure certainty of his artistic legitimacy, an assurance that the path he had chosen was not so outrageous as it seemed to his nineteenth-century critics. Isolated as Ensor was in Ostend from any of the rationalizing cliques with which the larger centers such as Paris and Brussels abounded in these years, this inspiration was the more significant and forceful.

Since 1883 he had worked mostly in the black and white of the drawings and prints and painted little, but now in the 1887 *St. Anthony* (page 66) and the Antwerp Museum's *Fall of the Rebellious Angels,* the exuberant, liberated, high-

Details, *Entry of Christ into Brussels in 1889*

Detail, *Entry of Christ into Brussels in 1889*

pitched color orchestration anticipates by a quarter of a century the freely slashed color of Kandinsky's "abstract expressionism."

The very size (about 8½ by 14 feet) of *The Entry of Christ into Brussels in 1889* (page 70), which Ensor painted in 1888, indicates the phenomenal boldness and energy which went into the creation of his major paintings during the next five years. The audacious nature of his conception is perhaps sufficiently indicated by the fact that the painting was not formally exhibited until the Ensor show in Brussels in 1929. The original reaction was so violent that it has become wholly clouded by legend. *Les XX,* though not with complete equanimity, exhibited Seurat's *Grande Jatte* in 1887, Gauguin in 1889, Cézanne and van Gogh in 1890,

The Entry of Christ into Brussels. 1898. Etching, 9¾ x 14″

and yet found it altogether impossible to show Ensor's *Entry*. And this is not surprising because it is in the truest sense a twentieth-century picture.

Faces quickly brought to life in a single sweep of a thick brush dipped into vivid color, multiply in a composition vibrant with pure, clear, and even harsh brilliance. The enormous canvas represents the whole contemporary Brussels world as it might come out into the streets to render gala homage to the entering Savior. The Christ himself, a tiny figure seated on an ass, is almost lost in the background. The real subject of the picture is the delirious mob, the soldiers, workers, rustics, the bourgeois around the platform in the foreground, who recognize this event as an occasion for the blaring horns of the town band and every sort of buffoonery.

The painting is endlessly fascinating in its details. Each head shocks the observer anew with the strength and directness and originality of its characterization. Beyond the immediate impact of the canvas, it is this power that causes the eye to move across it in slow discovery as though it were a written page on which each word must be understood. This is not to be confused with so-called literary art. Its terms are completely visual and the picture itself contains all the ambient necessary to its understanding. To find its equivalent one must go back to the compositions of such artists as Callot and Breugel. Unique in the nineteenth century, this picture pattern which is, as it were, to be "read," occurs again and again in Ensor's work.

Certainly the most original work in this group is the *Combat of Demons* (below), one of the forty-five etchings of 1888 during which Ensor also painted

Combat of Demons. 1888. Etching, 10⅜ x 12⅛″

Odd Insects (the Artist and Mme Ernest Rousseau). 1888. Etching, 4⅝ x 6¼″

The Terrible Sentinel. 1888. Etching, 7 x 9⅜″

Capture of a Strange City. 1888. Etching, 7 x 9⅜″

innumerable canvases in addition to the great *Entry*. In this print an extraordinary assortment of figures whirls around a page amazing for the freedom of imagination with which Ensor both invents his demons and describes their separate demoniac cruelties. The variety of demons, of posture, of expression, of weapons, fills the page to its corners with an almost breath-taking hysteria, in the very extravagance of which there is humor. And if Gauguin was just beginning the revolt towards a two-dimensional art in Paris in 1888, the figures of Ensor's *Combat of Demons* are set down flat upon the page with a fabulous inventiveness and an intoxication with line as movement and expression which make clear the appeal his works had for such an artist as Klee. Another 1888 print is a dark and irregularly bitten plate to which Ensor, with an extraordinary sense for the accidental effect, gave the title *Stars at the Cemetery* (page 78). Ensor is again and again more comprehensible in the twentieth-century context of expressionism and surrealism

Stars at the Cemetery. 1888.
Etching, 5½ x 7″

than he is in terms of the formal restraints of his own period. A painting which, like *The Entry of Christ into Brussels,* attempts to represent the artist's whole and considered personal vision of society, does not find any real successors until the appearance of such works as Picasso's *Guernica,* Peter Blume's *The Eternal City* or Tchelitchew's *Phenomena* in the middle of the 1930's.

Probably suggested by Balzac's story *Jesus Christ in Flanders,*[9] *The Entry* first appeared in Ensor's work in a large drawing of 1885: *Hail Jesus, King of the Jews* (page 68). In this and in the 1898 etching of the painting (page 74), we can read the slogans on the banners he was later largely to paint out on the canvas itself. "Les Charcutiers de Jerusalem," "Les Impressionistes Belges," "Phalange Wagner fracassant," "Colman's Mustard" . . . These, the "Fanfares Doctrinaires, toujour reussi" (sic), are the palms with which they honor the Christ. The painting vibrates with the imminent crucifixion.

The Entry of Christ into Brussels has rather broad political implications, although these are of a wholly negative character. Ensor was essentially apolitical in his thinking, and it is perhaps not without significance that among his drawings there is a sketch of Tolstoy made from a photograph. His small store of friends in this period was almost completely made up of socialist intellectuals, chief among them being Rops' son-in-law Eugène Demolder, who in 1891 published the first serious study of Ensor's work in *La Société Nouvelle,* a socialist review. Ensor himself was not untouched by the desperate wave of strikes that began in the mines

Skeletons Trying to Warm Themselves. 1889. Oil on canvas, 29½ x 23⅝". Collection Baron Robert Gendebien, Brussels

in 1886 and surged across Belgium during the next two years, to be put down with an official brutality that left five fishermen dead on the beach at Ostend. Several of his prints, notably *The Gendarmes,* which pointedly repeats Louis Gallait's composition of the murder of the Belgian heroes Egmont and Horn known to every Belgian school child, and the various versions of *Alimentation Doctrinaire* reflect the impact of these events.

But Ensor was never himself a socialist. He was too distrustful of the resources of mankind in any positive direction. Outside his art, James Ensor's life is actually a singular personal record of lack of event rather than event. The only alternative to a life whose very premises dismayed him was the death which would assuredly

Masks Confronting Death. 1888. Oil on canvas, 31½ x 39¼". Collection Gustave Van Geluwe, Brussels

Old Woman with Masks. 1889. Oil on canvas, 21⅝ x 18″. Collection Roland Leten, Ghent, Belgium

come to him whether he willed it or not. If he was born into a withering souvenir shop in Ostend, there he would remain, a torn lace curtain across the shop window when he died almost a century later — but the masks, the sea shells, the hatreds and the jokes of the shop transmuted by genius.[10]

Even today in Belgium such a recoil from life is never thought of as "neurotic," but simply as eccentric. Ensor relinquished life to become an observer. But like

Astonishment of the Mask Wouse. 1889. Oil on canvas, 42⅞ x 52". Royal Museum of Fine Arts, Antwerp

Dante's *Inferno,* his work now becomes a record of a descent into hell, a hell which is in this world, which completely encloses him, and from which there is no possible escape. Between 1888 and 1892 he paints a whole galaxy of carnival pictures which, like the earlier *Scandalized Masks,* admit the observer to fascinated participation in mysteriously menacing ritual.

The 1889 painting *Skeletons Trying to Warm Themselves* (page 79) is vividly characteristic of this group. The bleak room furnished only by a stove recalls the poverty of the earlier *Sick Tramp Warming Himself.* But now the open door of the stove shows only a cold blackness with the words, "pas de feu." The skeletons who have not even the sick tramp's poor flesh to keep them warm, huddle around it in their fantastic garments in an excruciating misery beyond the ordinary torments of this world. One thinks of T. S. Eliot's *Whispers of Immortality*—

> He knew the anguish of the marrow
> The ague of the skeleton;
> No contact possible to flesh
> Allayed the fever of the bone.

Cold and death—simple, universal affective elements. And yet on examination of the attributes, the palette, the violin, and the lamp of the three skeletons in the foreground, it becomes probable that Ensor's painting must have begun as an allegory of the life of the artist, the musician, and the writer. This complete subordination of the idea to the picture's emotional impact on the observer is characteristic of Ensor in the late 1880's as it is characteristic of the twentieth-century surrealist movement. His works are compounded out of the personal and the local, but they always proceed from some tangible experience with an inner logic and integrity which can be sensed even when its more immediate starting point is not explicitly definable in terms of the facts at hand.

The challenge of mystery becomes part of the fascination of these paintings. The wanton relationship between human beings in the Antwerp Museum's 1890 *Intrigue* (page 21) is immediately sensed in the electric definition of the painting. And this is indeed a tribute to Ensor's art, to his ability to project the personal and the local in universally significant and affective terms. For in the language of the carnival, the *intrigue* of the title represents the acting out of some local scandal in a kind of charade by the masked revellers. The man and woman in the center are the main actors in this drama. The mask of the woman, with its upturned eyes and mouth hanging open, wears a look of almost idiotic ecstasy; she wears white flowers and hangs on the arm of the man like a new bride. The man wears a top hat and half hides his expressionless oriental mask in the fur collar of his coat. These merciless figures mock the marriage of Ensor's own sister to a Chinese who kept an art shop in Berlin, and whom she left after a year to live in Ostend with her daughter. The woman in the foreground of the painting holds a little oriental doll and points to the man with a gloved hand which is given emphasis by its color.

None of this information is necessary to the appreciation of *Intrigue,* the essence of which is pinned vividly to the canvas with the bright blues and reds. Yet, however mysterious Ensor's fantasies may seem, no one of this group is without its base in an acute reality. The mechanics of the transformation process are in many ways similar to the mechanics of humor and its success is similarly measured by the brilliance with which it illuminates the subject. Ensor's was the quick insight, the extraordinary genius for this brilliant and bitter pageant which breaks through the limiting boundaries of art-for-art's-sake to find a personal but convincing symbolism.

This is far from the deliberate mystifications of Odilon Redon, who was bringing the essence of symbolist poetry into the visual arts. The following passage from a Redon letter of 1898 discussing his 1882 series of Poe lithographs, indicates a peculiar irresponsibility with regard to subject, and is a tribute only to the power Poe's name had become in France.

> All the reasons that I will give you for the textual sources of my albums will seem to you insignificant and childish. They simply provide them with the prestige they

Skeletons Disputing a Herring (hareng-saur/art Ensor). 1891. Oil on panel, 6¼ x 8½". Collection Benedict Goldschmidt, Brussels

Murder. 1890. Oil on canvas, 23⅝ x 30″. Collection Marcel Mabille, Brussels

> had to have. Once again, it is good to surround every genesis with a mystery. When I undertook the . . . work, *To Edgar Poe,* I had, alas, lost all my innocence . . . I had many times been advised to read the American poet as offering a precedent for my art. The advisors were, I believe, mistaken; his tales are hardly my favorite reading. Nevertheless, I place a few words under these new prints, aptly, I believe, and the public fools itself. Obviously, I went no further than an allowable equivocation, very legitimate; the album was noted, that was the essential for me.[11]

This element of deliberate obfuscation was to multiply in twentieth-century surrealism, was finally to kill it as the exigencies of events created a seriousness of atmosphere in which an artist like Ensor, who is by contrast the provincial moralist, seems more relevant.

Forbidding Figure (Portrait of the Artist's Aunt). 1890. Oil on panel, 9⅝ x 7½". Collection Marcel Mabille, Brussels

Ensor's meaning is intensely conveyed even where the separate elements are not specifically identifiable. *The Astonishment of the Mask Wouse* (page 82) stems from some incident of the carnival. Masks and costumes are strewn about the floor, abandoned with the clarinet, the violin and the skull. Two hideous visages peer into the scene from the frame, spirits, perhaps, watching over the dead carnival, its harsh brilliance, its ugly cruelty, its mortality. Into this room the Mask Wouse enters, stretching out a bony claw in surprise. These are her comrades and her world stretched out here on the floor. Still she remains, a skeleton to support the trappings of the carnival, holding an umbrella which seems to represent the determination with which she will continue nevertheless to maintain herself and the complete abandonment of hope and dignity of which her dripping nose is the hideous sign.

This is the marrow of Ensor's many carnival paintings during this period. The 1891 *Skeletons Fighting for the Body of a Hanged Man* (page 19), is not a battle of good against evil. The hanged man has lost all of his humanity and watches his own doom with a buffoonish satisfaction. The masks watch avidly from the doorway with excited sadistic delight. It is a lively and gaudy show and it is Ensor's own tortured sense of the mob's mortality. Whichever skeleton wins, the fate is death. Like *Gulliver's Travels* it is a testament of horror that has all the elements of an amusement for children.

Carnival is mankind at its most vile and its most colorful. Like Swift, Ensor was

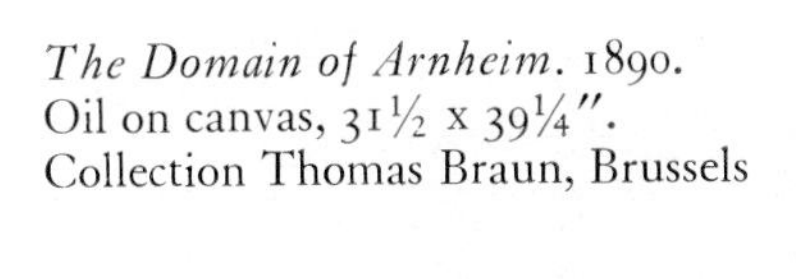

The Domain of Arnheim. 1890.
Oil on canvas, 31½ x 39¼".
Collection Thomas Braun, Brussels

Farm at Leffinghe. 1889. Etching, 3⅛ x 4⅝″

Wind. 1888. Etching, 7 x 9¾″

The Street Lamp. 1888. Etching, 3¾ x 2¾″

Woods at Groenendael. 1888. Etching, 4⅝ x 3¾″

Shrimp. 1894. Private collection, Brussels

tormented by the cruel stupidities of human existence. Unlike Swift, he never succumbed to madness, persisted to the same notable old age as his Flemish forebears, a relic of a generation whose artists and writers had mostly tortured themselves into early graves. Ensor was sustained by a deep well of sheer vitality, an invigorating delight in the color and movement and infinite shapes of the world. It is this two-way sensibility that makes the morbidity of these carnival paintings bearable and makes them great works of art. A painting like *Woman Eating Oysters* is emblematic of the robust sensual apparatus typical of Flanders, incarnate in Rubens, Jordaens, Snyders, and in Ensor. His still lifes of the 1880's are alert with a joyous satisfaction in the rich abundance of nature: glowing fruits, cabbages and celeries, feathery fowl, nacreous oysters. From his studio window he paints the streets and roofs and sky of Ostend with enchanted pleasure. A painting like the 1887 *Carnival on the Beach* (page 15) is a luminous haze of light that surpasses even Turner's radiance.

Turner is suggested again in certain of Ensor's landscapes, notably the 1890 *Domain of Arnheim* (page 87). *Carnival on the Beach* has as well a formal and unworldly loveliness that in the *Garden of Love,* which follows now in a darker park-like setting, shimmers with a brilliance that rather recalls Monticelli, whom Ensor was later to call a "powerful inspiration . . . the alchemist of rubies, of emeralds, of sapphires, and of gold."

The Watteau theme of the *Garden of Love* was to be repeated again and again in Ensor's later work with a gay, ballet-like and mocking grace. Love was a

Shells. 1895. Oil on canvas, 39½ x 32″. Collection Baron de Broqueville, Brussels

beguiling fancy to be lightly burlesqued. In 1907 he began work on an actual ballet, *The Game of Love,* for which he composed the scenario and music as well as the decor, and this was produced in Brussels in 1920.[12]

One of Ensor's earliest literary essays, the 1884 *Three Weeks at the Academy* is already cast in dramatic form. The stage is important in connection with his art. The devices of horizontality, movement in from both sides of the painting as from the wings of a stage, the close back wall which permits a simple suggestion of setting, all recall this source. But more basic than these is a certain theatrical quality in the conception of all the works. In contrast to the impressionists' attempt

The Tower of Lisseweghe. 1888. Oil on canvas, 24 x 28¾". Collection Franck

Boats. 1890. Oil on canvas, 24⅜ x 26¾". Royal Museum of Fine Arts, Antwerp

to achieve a natural and casual representation, Ensor's work has in common with the theater the deliberate introduction or elimination of elements with reference to a calculated effect on the observer, and the wide variety of his techniques suggests the impresario who is always ready to adopt a new style if it will render the work at hand more vividly effective. The subject is always the starting point. Painting and etching, impressionism and expressionism, color subtly monotone or harshly vibrant, natural landscape panorama, space frankly abstract and artificial — Ensor is both the colorist and the draughtsman and his gamut runs the whole scale from outright caricature to conceptions of the most consummate elegance and refine-

Music, Rue de Flandre. 1891. Oil on panel, 9½ x 7½″. Royal Museum of Fine Arts, Antwerp

ment. Even in the twentieth century his diversity seems extraordinary, and he was far from the formal restraints of his own period. ". . . Yes, before me the painter did not heed his vision . . . Limited spirits demand constant recommencements, repetitions . . . odiously classify artists like bedded oysters."[13] . . . "All rules, all canons of art, vomit death."[14]

White and Red Clowns Evolving. 1890. Drawing in color, 9½ x 11½". Collection Benedict Goldschmidt, Brussels

"DEMONS TORMENTING ME" — 1892-1898

The "limited spirits" had their own revenge. In 1882, with his showing at the Paris Salon, Ensor had sold *Chinoiseries* and *Bourgeois Salon*. A year later the Ostend collector who had bought them was frightened by the critics' sharp attacks and hung the paintings in the Ostend casino, hoping at least to get his money back. The canvases remained there with their for-sale signs for six or seven years. Finally the devoted Ernest Rousseau who was rector of Brussels University, bought *Bourgeois Salon*, and Ensor's mother retrieved *Chinoiseries* for 65 francs from a second-hand dealer who had taken it in exchange for a table.

Christ in Hell. 1891. Drawing, 8¾ x 11¾″. Mlle Julienne Boogaerts

Small Persian Torture. 1893 (?). Colored drawing on paper, 8¼ x 9½″. Collection Mlle Julienne Boogaerts, Brussels

The few works which Ensor did sell in the ensuing years went for trifling and humiliating sums. After the row in *Les XX* over the exhibition of *The Entry of Christ into Brussels* in 1889, Ensor was not even certain of a showing with this group, and after 1894 when Maus supplanted the artist directorate and it became *La Libre Esthétique,* he was only an occasional exhibitor.

There was not the desperate poverty of van Gogh. Ensor was comfortable enough in his studio high up over the souvenir shop, an odd figure of a man in his mother's house, butt to the peasant jokes of Ostend. But a sense of outrage chokes light and color out of many of the figure compositions of the middle 90's. *The Bad Doctors* (page 100) of 1895 is conceived on a level where one is surprised that the inscribed

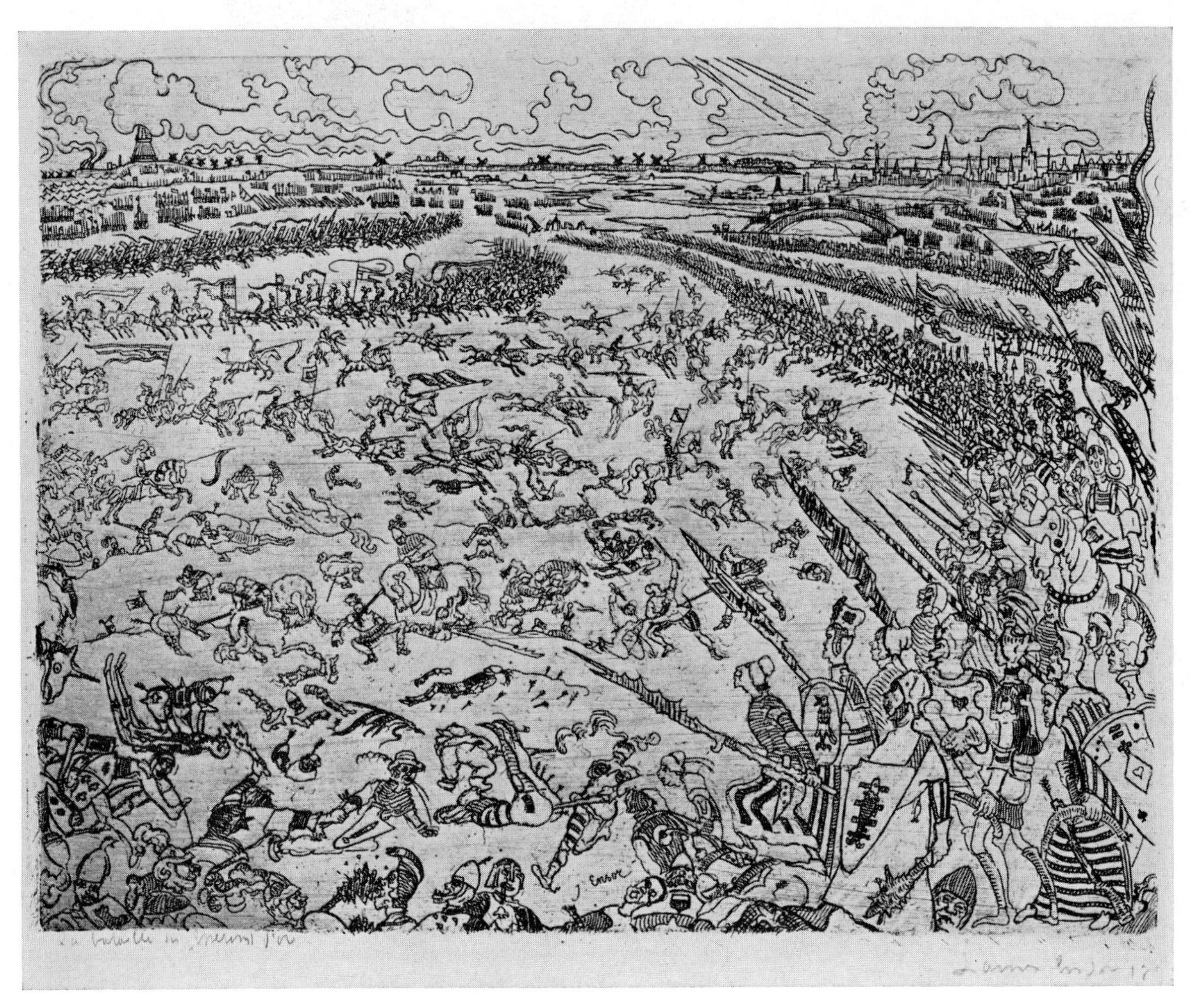

The Battle of the Golden Spurs. 1895. Etching, 7 x 9½"

Death Pursuing the People. 1896. Etching, $9\frac{3}{8}$ x $7\frac{1}{4}$″

The Scavenger. 1896. Etching, hand-colored in watercolor by the artist, 4¾ x 3¼″. Collection Mlle Julienne Boogaerts, Brussels

sarcasms do not balloon out of the mouths of the figures. The esthetic of the affective equivalent is here relinquished for an uncontrolled exaggeration which leaves the observer uncertainly amused at the wild dismemberment of the sick man.

There is a succession of these mettlesome farces. The 1896 *Dangerous Cooks* (page 101) is a strange cartoon to find elaborated in oils on canvas. One of the cooks is Octave Maus who is about to serve a herring who has Ensor's head *(hareng saur — art Ensor)* to the critics Fétis, Demolder, Lemonnier, Sulzberger and Verhaeren who are seated at a table in the next room. The other cook is Edmond Picard, who is represented as frying the head of the painter Vogels, while the heads of Lemmen and Van Rysselberghe wait on the shelf, and the head of the painter Anna Boch with the body of a chicken hangs from a string. Théo Hannon essays

Fridolin and Gragapança of Yperdam. 1895. Etching, 4 x 5⅝″

The Bad Doctors. 1895. Etching, 7 x 9 ⅞″

The Judges. 1894. Etching, 7⅛ x 9⅜″

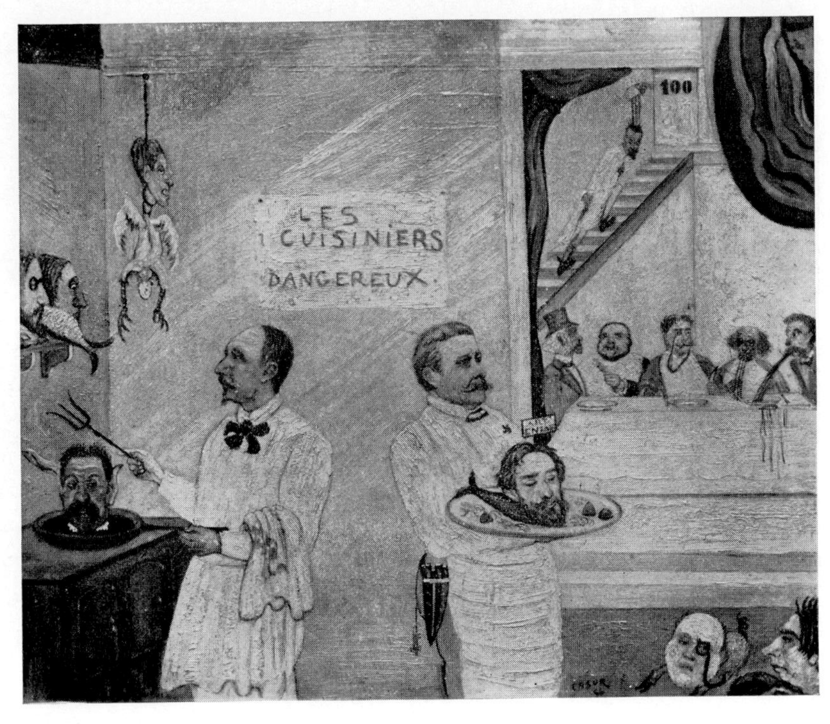

Dangerous Cooks. 1896. Oil on panel, 15 x 18⅛″. Collection Roland Leten, Ghent

Poster for exhibition in Paris under the auspices of *La Plume*. 1898. Colored lithograph, 21 x 14¾″

Demons Tormenting Me. 1895. Etching, 4⅝ x 6⅛″

Demons Tormenting Me. 1888.
Drawing, 8⅝ x 11¾″.
Collection Mlle Julienne Boogaerts,
Brussels

the staircase at the back, but gets a chamber pot emptied on his head.

A *blague* to amuse the artist's friends and irritate his critics, the etching *The Judges* (page 101) repeats substantially the same theme. Ensor again confronts his critics who are now seen in the caps and gowns of the law courts. They are arranged behind a table on which an amputated human leg, teeth, and various butcher knives mingle with the inkwells. The artist stands before this tribunal with two criminals (the two thieves of the crucifixion?) in an open-mouthed harangue whose intensity is indicated by the drops of sweat which pour from his face.

Demolder wrote: "The art of Ensor . . . was an art of battle . . . it has become an art of exasperation." Even some of the still lifes begin to reflect the tensions of this period. The 1882 *Skate* in the Antwerp Museum is a fish turned out of a basket on glistening straw. *The Skate* of 1892 (page 23) is not so much a fish as a strange and inscrutable sea monster. With the 1889 *Attributes of the Studio* (page 17) Ensor had broken still-life tradition in that the masks become actual presences. In the 90's even some of his more conventional still-life paintings supplant the earlier fruits, vegetables, fish and fowl with an emphasis on bottles, painted crockery and china, metal candlesticks, sea shells, crabs and lobsters, objects all strangely hard and unyielding, and suggesting only the calcine remnants of life, which are represented by the scavenger crustaceans. The painting itself is hard and brilliant, and it is a savage genius that succeeds in rendering even the still life weirdly suggestive of unrelenting death.

Many of the prints of the middle 90's return to earlier sources of inspiration. In 1895 Ensor etches *The Sick Tramp Warming Himself* (from the painting of 1882), *Christ Tormented by Demons* (from the drawing dated 1888), *Battle of the Golden Spurs* (from the drawing of 1891), *Skeletons Trying to Warm Themselves* (from the painting of 1889), *Scandalized Masks* (from the painting of 1883), *King Pest* (from the drawing dated 1880). *Demons Tormenting Me* (page 103) is from a drawing dated 1888. Ensor's dates on some of the drawings and paintings were inscribed many years after memory could be trusted, and certain of these dates are surely dubious. But his work is a rich and tangled skein of concurrent styles, and it is often exactly the dating of the extraordinary prefigurations one is most inclined to suspect that is substantiated by early exhibition catalogues.

The drawing for the 1896 print *Death Pursuing the People* (page 98) is dated 1882. Humanity — the woman with a child, soldiers, clergy, police, a grinning man with monocle and top hat, bonneted peasants — is crushed in panic between the high walls of houses on a narrow street, each individual trapped by the presence of all the others, a man in the right foreground slaughtering those about him in his

Portrait of the Artist Surrounded by Masks. 1899. Oil on canvas, 47¼ x 31½″.
Collection Cléomire Jussiant, Antwerp

Skeletons Playing Billiards. 1903. Drawing, 9½ x 11¾″. Collection Marcel Mabille, Brussels

Anger (The Seven Deadly Sins series). 1904. Etching, 3⅞ x 5⅞″

effort to break free. There is no possible escape from the hideous death who floats above the mob brandishing his scythe; those who have remained within their houses are only served by fire and by lesser demons.

In 1896 Guernica and Hiroshima were only the picturesque names of far-off places, but if *Death Pursuing the People* (page 98) seems a strange foreshadowing of events to come almost half a century later, it also has its tradition in such a painting as Breugel's *Triumph of Death* in the Prado, which is closely parodied in Ensor's 1913 drawing *War of the Snails* (page 113). There is a correspondence between Ensor's vision here and the northern Gothic sense of the world as alive with the agents of Hell which the individual must overcome to save his soul. The 1895 *Demons Tormenting Me* is in a convention that departs very little from such a work as Martin Schongauer's *St. Anthony* engraving (page 122) which Ensor would have seen in the Brussels Museum.

Within this tradition Ensor now projects his experience with a broad and effective significance he does not achieve in his wholly original caricatures of himself and his critics. But the fact that the artist finds a strengthening framework in tradition does not mean that he himself contributes nothing to that tradition. A sense of the past is a sense of the future because it is a sense of the continuity of life. *Death Pursuing the People* is closer to Picasso's *Guernica* than it is to Breugel. In *Demons Tormenting Me,* Ensor's demons begin to suggest the nightmarish and half-pathetic grotesques of such surrealists as Ernst, Picabia, and Masson. The many-eyed man and the many-breasted woman are themselves the pitiful aberrations of an irresponsible creation.

THE MONUMENT IN OSTEND

In 1896 Demolder organized a show of Ensor's work in Brussels, and as a result of this exhibition *The Lamp Boy,* which had been painted sixteen years before when the artist was twenty, was acquired by the Brussels Museum. In 1898 there was the exhibition in Paris under the auspices of the review *La Plume,* with the special numbers of the magazine reproducing many of Ensor's works. The poster for this exhibition (page 102), a color lithograph, is a new version of *Demons Tormenting Me,* in which the earlier tombstone reading "J. Ensor 1895" gives way to a triumphant cock. This is in the curvilinear *art nouveau* style of French posters of this period, a style that Ensor occasionally uses exuberantly in his drawings around the turn of the century.

An unsigned article in *L'Art Moderne* at the time Ensor's paintings were refused by the Brussels Salon in 1884, remarks: "All of his canvases have been refused . . .

Double Portrait (The Artist and Mlle Augusta Boogaerts). 1905. Oil on panel, 15½ x 13″. Collection Mlle Julienne Boogaerts, Brussels

perhaps one might say that this intransigent spirit pleases himself in exaggerating difficulties, choosing among his productions those which seem to him most likely to provoke rage, red for the bulls invested with the right to judge them. They strike at him bellowing with horns lowered. This is droll, but understandable. Whether it is wise or just is another question."

Ensor had not wanted to be shown for his diplomacy, but for his genius. The more intransigent he was, the greater would be the triumph of that genius. The 1889 painting *Old Woman with Masks* (page 81) began as a commission from a well-meaning Belgian who brought Ensor a photograph of his dead wife from which he wanted a portrait painted. Ensor did not refuse; he agreed, and painted a picture to end all such commissions. Of course it was not accepted, and remained one of the delights of the artist's studio until the 40's. It is a splendid painting, it is a revelation — and it is a pitiless joke.

Ensor's genius was a driving need to bring the world into focus, and what he saw was far from agreeable pleasantries to be indulged in by the rich as a piece of conspicuous consumption. But that genius was stronger even than his perversity, and after the success in Paris in 1898 his most difficult time was past. Even before 1914 rich collections of his prints were formed in Germany, and the first catalogue of his prints was published by Garvens-Garvensburg in Hanover in 1913. The Austrian expressionist Alfred Kubin owned many of the prints. In the rubbish of the studio after Ensor's death, were two 1912 lithographs by Paul Klee,[15] who must certainly have given or sent them to the artist whose reputation for closeness was famous and deserved. Klee sometimes used an Ensor composition in the same way that an artist uses a model, and as Ensor himself used compositions by Callot and others. During the 1914-1918 German occupation of Belgium, Ensor remained in Ostend although most of his friends and family fled across the channel to England, and he received many visits from German artists during this period.

In the years between the two wars James Ensor became a kind of political shuttlecock: the French held Ensor exhibitions in Paris to demonstrate their solidarity with the Belgians, while at the same time the Germans were pointing out that their own affinity for Ensor and for Belgian art was not political or conventional but rather spiritual and almost biological. Actually through his father Ensor was a British subject until 1929 when he was made a baron by the Belgian King, but the English have not been quick to claim him. The Belgians themselves cautiously followed Paris in honoring the strange prophet they had produced. In 1903 Ensor was named a Chevalier of the Order of Leopold, but it was the neo-impressionist Théo Van Rysselberghe whom Octave Maus invited to represent Belgium at *La Libre Esthétique's* Salon of Innovators in 1904. As late as the articles

Decor for the artist's ballet, *The Game of Love*. 1914. Oil on canvas, 66⅛ x 81⅛". Collection J. Janssen, Antwerp

following the baronetcy of 1929 the critics emphasize the point that they prefer the earliest style of the 1880's, and it was not until after the recent war that the later works soared in the sharp Brussels art market as a safe investment for money.

In the *Portrait of the Artist Surrounded by Masks* (page 105) Ensor wears plumes and flowers on his hat. Not, as in the 1883 *Flowered Hat* (page 43), as a youthful challenge to Rubens, but because almost visibly in this 1899 self portrait he becomes a mask himself. A mask in the midst of masks. In the foreground these are predominantly gay. Behind the artist, and in sharply diminishing perspective, are the cruel skulls, the hideous grimaces and leers. He turns his back on them, but they are relentlessly present.

Ensor was actually only thirty-eight at the time of the *La Plume* exhibition, though it is true that he had been painting for more than two decades. In his 1922 monograph, the Belgian poet Grégoire Le Roy paints a sad picture of the artist as already a white-bearded old man at the time of this recognition in 1898. Neither the self portraits nor photographs of the period bear this out, but it was a fiction

Detail, *The Game of Love*

Delights of Winter. 1914. Drawing. Collection Mme Richard Daveluy, Ostend

War of the Snails. 1913. Colored drawing, 16⅜ x 18⅛″. Collection Benedict Goldschmidt, Brussels

that Ensor himself promoted with delight. Success had its own elements of carnival, now ridiculous rather than cruel. His last revenge against the hated mob was to play the old clown just as it was ready to accept him as hero.

> Grizzled in the service of my multiple fantasies, I am infected with respectability. In my twenties, young ladies turned away from me nobly; now they smile at me with all their teeth.[16]

Not only young ladies, but critics and collectors. Ensor was to live on for another half-century, to work up until the drawings of the early 1940's. And the works of these years are a gigantic and deliberate mockery which is still more comfortably snubbed as the antics of an enfeebled old man. The artist himself now collaborated with the carnival by playing the silly old fool in whom the fires of youth are dead,

The Artist's Mother in Death. 1915. Oil, 7¼ x 9½″. Collection Mme Richard Daveluy, Ostend

whose recognition had come too late. As late as 1930, André de Ridder notes "a certain remission after the great period 1880-1886" — or before the *Entry* of 1888 and what are now seen to be Ensor's most important and original works. The outstanding monograph of the 1940's notes discreetly, "He [Ensor] does not conceal from himself certain weaknesses of his production after 1900." Ensor's is a whole history of being always far ahead of critical comprehension, and one should be cautious about being taken in by his late mask of capricious senility.

If he had been the tormented Gulliver among the Yahoos, he was now marooned in Lilliput, and with Alice's magic ability to participate in small mad tea parties and games. The skeletons are no longer trying to warm themselves; they play at billiards in comic exuberance, careless of their reduced state. Recognition had relieved the tension and detached the artist from the ferocious battle, and it was part of his genius not to say again what he had already said so magnificently, but rather to put it all in a whole new way. He had, so to speak, "lost his passion," but an enormously rich, imaginative, and pointedly sardonic humor remained — a more successful defense, a new weapon; Freud's definition of humor as simultaneous aggression and regression is pertinent.

The number, the variety, and the elaborate comic extravagance of Ensor's works until the early 40's, indicate that the artist was far from enfeebled. If a falsetto is sounded, it is a deliberate falsetto; even the still lifes of this period, pastel, dry, linear, are made to parody life.

The work of the early century abounds in large illustrational projects. *Skeletons Playing Billiards* (page 106) is one of a group of compositions called *The History of Billiards.* The *Seven Deadly Sins* series was completed in 1904. On the appointment as a Chevalier of the Order of Leopold, came the fantastic drawings for *Les Ecus,* subtitled "Discourse by James Ensor in the Noble Language of Chivalry." In the grotesque 1912 series of *Scenes from the Life of Christ,* the *Baptism* typically becomes a farce of two bathers one of whom douses the other from a wash bucket, and reminds one that the 1887 St. Anthony had already appeared as a bewildered figure who seems hardly to understand the significance of his experience. This series was reproduced mechanically on lithograph stones and published in 1921. The 1911 costume sketches for Ensor's ballet *The Game of Love* were similarly published in color in 1929, with Ensor's scenario, music, and a reproduction of the large 1914 painting which sets the scene for the second act (page 110).

The Game of Love is subtitled *Flirt des Marionettes.* Beyond the masks, humanity in Ensor's late work becomes a species of fantastically motivated puppets in a studied and remorseless denial of any sense or dignity in man's fate. The artist himself appears again and again, the leading figure in this new Punch and Judy, a little white cotton-whiskered mannikin in an insistent "state of decay."

He takes up quixotic campaigns against vivisection, and for the protection of the dunes of the coast which were being obliterated by hotels and boardwalks. But the overwhelming preoccupation is with his own fame, his own triumphant challenge to death. He hugs the early work: refuses to sell it, signs it, sometimes several

Droll Smokers. c.1920. Oil on canvas, 29½ x 25¼". Collection Mlle Julienne Boogaerts, Brussels

times, dates it, copies it, elaborates the titles, colors early etchings, sketches paintings in little copy-books, with their histories written in a minuscule hand. The paintings hang in the house as part of the scenery of his life, to figure again and again in the later canvases. The 1930 *Studio of the Artist* (page 120) in the Boymans Museum in Rotterdam represents a corner of the studio in which the 1889 *Old Woman with Masks* and the great *Entry of Christ* can be recognized. Through a doorway, small and remote, the artist himself is visible. Ensor's whole history is contained in this corner of the studio; the tiny, puppet-like ancient in the background is a small, but pointed, part of that history.

Ensor's fantastic writings, which fill a thick volume in the collected edition of 1944, mostly date from this post-1900 period and constitute another mocking salute to his own genius. Originating as essays for local journals, or speeches at the recurrent banquets which were a feature of Belgian art life before the recent war, these are wittily corrosive characterizations of other artists and of critics, or even more cleverly destructive flattery of those who happen to be present. And above all, ". . . Well before Vuillard, Bonnard, van Gogh and the luminists, I indicated all the modern experiments, all the influence of light, the liberation of vision."[17] . . . "When I look at my drawings of 1877 I find cubist angles, futurist explosions,

Banquet of the Starved. c.1925. Oil on canvas, 45⅛ x 57⅜". Collection Miss Adelaide M. deGroot, New York

Page from notebook. 1937. Pencil, 8⅝ x 7⅛″. Curt Valentin, New York

impressionist flakings, dada knights and constructivist structures."[18] Much of this was justified, and it is couched in a tinseled and inventive sequence of untranslatable sound and phrase. Ensor apparently never read Swift, and this is a pity; he would have found in the Dubliner even more of himself than he found in Poe; Ensor adored words like "Houyhnhnm" and "Brobdingnag."[19]

His mother died in 1915, but Ensor lived on in a house above a souvenir shop with two servants who were almost as old as himself. As the house became more and more a place of pilgrimage for visitors to the Belgian coast, Ensor and the manservant Auguste conspired in a kind of sideshow performance which was repeated for visitor after visitor. One was admitted by Auguste in a blue apron and a red Turk's cap, and followed him up a dark stairway to the room of haunted furniture, to be presented to the Master in his armchair by the window. Ensor was a really beautiful old man, with a pink freshness of skin and soft whiteness of hair and beard, and he was always elegant for these visits in a black suit, an old-fashioned bow tie, and the black Homburg hat which, like a peasant, he always wore in his house. Now the whole company ascended another floor to the studio,

My Austere Visage Lighted by Moons. 1937. Oil on panel, 13¼ x 10". Collection Mr. and Mrs. Harry J. Rudick, New York

The Studio of the Artist. c.1930. Oil on canvas, 26 x 33″. Collection D. G. Van Beuningen, Vierhouten, Gelderland, The Netherlands

to admire the great *Entry of Christ* and the paintings, the masks and the sea shells grouped like fetishes. Finally Ensor would play his own compositions on the harmonium or the piano while the flattered visitor mused. No one was admitted before four o'clock, and inspired critics left the house in the lovely twilight of Ostend to go home and publish this same interview in French, German, English, Dutch, and undoubtedly several other languages. In 1946, Auguste had added a fascinating finale: as he descended the staircase to show the visitor to the door, he went backwards out of consideration for the rheumatism in his legs, and the visitor left more than ever convinced that he had touched Ensor's very soul.

Ensor, in little or no disguise, is the hero in at least three novels and one play published around 1900.[20] For Demolder he becomes a figure in Flemish folklore; for Picard, a baffling reincarnation of Bosch; for French Jean Lorrain a Baudelairian sophisticate in search of sensation. Much of the enormous critical literature in French and German is equally contradictory and irrelevant. Ensor is indeed an elusive phenomenon, too isolated, too independent, too varied and complex to be easily assimilable into the history of art. He is among the most original of artists, but this is partly an instinct for sources of inspiration even more extraordinary in the nineteenth century than it seems in the twentieth. At home in Ostend in the 80's and 90's James Ensor is in a certain sense the first artist in Malraux' *Imaginary Museum*. Rubens, Hals, Rembrandt, Callot, Turner, Breugel, Gallait and de Braekeleer, Schongauer, pass through his hands with the swift demonology of the Japanese printmaker Kuniyoshi, to become ineluctably Ensorian. His paintings, drawings and prints are ultimately their own splendid power. But beyond that, they announce and to a considerable extent actually shape twentieth-century expressionism and surrealism. The formative influence of Ensor's works on Klee, on such artists as Nolde, Kubin, Chagall, on such a Belgian as Delvaux, is direct and obvious.

Fantastic art is a peculiar comcomitant of a world at war. Both the Callot of the *Miseries of War* series and the Goya of *The Disasters of War* have also left us a series called *Caprices*. The world without morality or order reaches beyond the logic of tragedy to its own wild grotesque comedy. In this middle of the twentieth century, Ensor's meanings are clear and unmistakable; his fantasies seem more literal than fantastic.

NOTES TO THE TEXT

1. "Notre corps . . . nous donne l'exemple d'une dégringolade à partir de la vingtième année. Nous sommes faits pour descendre et non pas pour monter. Mais le génie nous sauvera." Quoted by Firmin Cuypers in *James Ensor, l'homme et l'oeuvre,* Paris, Les Ecrivains réunis, 1925. pp. 13, 14

2. "Je veux parler longtemps encore aux hommes de demain." Ensor letter reproduced by Albert Croquez in *L'Oeuvre gravé de James Ensor,* Paris, Maurice Le Garrec, 1935. p. iii

3. Reproduced in L. Dumont-Wilden, *F. Khnopff,* Brussels, 1907, facing p. 14. Verhaeren (*James Ensor*, Brussels, Van Oest, 1908, p. 22) notes the influence of Ensor on the early work of both Khnopff and the Dutch painter Jan Toorop, who was also a member of *Les XX*. For the work of the latter see Plasschaert, *Jan Toorop,* Amsterdam, 1925.

4. Quoted by Florent Fels in *Propos d'Artistes,* Paris, Renaissance du Livre, 1925. p. 56

5. Quoted by André de Ridder in *Chroniques du jour,* Paris, 1930. p. 31

6. This sentence appears again and again in Ensor's writings as a kind of signature or *leitmotif*. It is a reference to the fable of the frog who puffed himself up till he burst.

7. Marius Vachon, *Jacques Callot,* Paris, Librairie de l'art, 1886 (Les artistes célèbres, v.9)

8. There is a painting of *The Vengeance of Hop Frog,* and a lithograph as well as the etching. Ensor's composition is clearly inspired by the setting of Callot's *Le Premier Intermède* (Lieure 185). It is even closer to the Callot drawing of this scene in the collection of the Berlin Kupferstichkabinett (reproduced Hermann Nasse, *Jacques Callot,* Leipzig, n.d., Pl. 5a), but it is not possible to say how or where Ensor might have seen this.

9. Ensor actually mentions this Balzac story in his *Ecrits, 1921-26* (IVe Cahier de "La Flandre Littéraire"), Ostende-Bruges, 1926. p. 22

10. "Countries differ in aspect, in climate, in atmosphere, in temperature, and always one senses a secret accord between a man and his surroundings. In the eyes of a painter, the pole is very far from the equator. Fast travel multiplies, and soon men will cross whole nations without seeing them. But always it will be necessary for men to build their houses, fish their fishes, cultivate their gardens, plant their cabbages, and for that they must see with all their eyes. And to see is to paint, and to paint is to love—nature and woman and children and the solid earth." Ensor letter reproduced p. 3, *Ecrits, 1921-26*

11. *Lettres d'Odilon Redon, 1878-1916,* Paris and Brussels, G. Van Oest, 1923. p. 31

12. Ensor's ballet was again produced in Antwerp in 1924, in Liège in 1927, at Ostend in 1932, in Ghent and Tournai in 1936. As a young man, the artist played the flute (see *Fridolin and Gragapança of Yperdam,* page 100). Later in life, he was fondest of the piano and the harmonium. Besides his ballet, Ensor composed several shorter musical pieces—among them a *March for the Rotarians.*

MARTIN SCHONGAUER:
Saint Anthony. Engraving. *Cf. pp. 102, 103*

13. *Les Ecrits de James Ensor,* Editions "Sélection," Brussels, 1921. pp. 23, 24

14. *Ecrits 1921-26.* p. 13

15. These were *Tragedy on Stilts* and *Street-Urchins,* both reproduced by H. von Wedderkop in *Paul Klee,* Leipzig, 1920 (Junge Kunst series, bd. 13)

16. *Ecrits 1921-26.* p. 7

17. *Ecrits,* 1921. p. 23

18. *Ecrits 1921-26.* p. 21

19. Ensor's father was himself born in Brussels, and lived most of his life on the Continent. The painter always spoke French (rather than the Flemish which is also current in Ostend), and at least in his late years his English consisted only of a variety of phrases like "Chicken in the Basket" and "You are a splendid donkey."

20. The novels are *Le royaume authentique du grand Saint Nicolas,* by Eugène Demolder, Paris, Ed. du Mercure de France, n.d.; *Histoire mirifique de Saint Dodon,* by Maurice des Ombiaux, Paris, Ollendorff, 1899; *Monsieur de Phocas,* by Jean Lorrain, Paris, Ollendorff, 1901; the play is Edmond Picard's *Psuké,* Brussels, Lacomblez, 1903.

SELECTED BIBLIOGRAPHY

Compiled by Hannah B. Muller, *Assistant Librarian, The Museum of Modern Art, New York*

Included are references to the most significant and accessible material on Ensor. For additional indications, the bibliographies mentioned below (bibl. 21, 32, 34, 42) should be consulted, as well as such sources as Thieme-Becker: *Allgemeines Lexikon der bildenden Künstler,* v. 10, Leipzig, Seemann, 1914, and the *Art Index,* New York, H. W. Wilson, 1929-51.

Items preceded by a dagger (†) have not been examined by the compiler, and the citation, therefore, may be incomplete.

ENSOR'S MAJOR WRITINGS AND ILLUSTRATIONS

1 Scènes de la vie du Christ, Bruxelles, Galerie Georges Giroux, 1921, 3p. plus 32 col. plates

2 Les Écrits de James Ensor, Bruxelles, Editions Sélection, 1921, 161p., illus.

3 Écrits . . . de 1921 à 1926, Ostende-Bruges, Éditions de "La Flandre littéraire," 1926, 32p., illus. (IVe cahier de La Flandre littéraire)
With an introduction by Firmin Cuypers

4 La Gamme d'amour, Bruxelles, Éditions du Coup de Dés, 1929, 11p. plus 22 col. plates
German translation in Paul Westheim: Künstlerbekenntnisse, Berlin, Propyläen Verlag, n.d., p. 36-41

5 Les Écrits de James Ensor (1928-1934), Anvers, L'Art Contemporain, 1934, 112p., 2 illus. plus col. plate

6 Les Écrits de James Ensor, Bruxelles, Éditions de la Lumière, 1944, 265p., illus. (Collection "Témoignages," v. 1)
Introduction by Henri Vandeputte. Includes material contained in bibl. 2, 3, 5

See also 11, 15, 44, 58

CATALOGUES OF ENSOR'S PRINTS

7 Croquez, Albert. L'oeuvre gravé de James Ensor. Catalogue raisonné, Paris, Le Garrec, 1935, 49p., port.
Lists 133 works

8 ———L'oeuvre gravé de James Ensor, Genève-Bruxelles, Pierre Cailler, 1947, 24p., illus. (ports.) plus 137 plates (some col.)
Lists 133 works

9 Delteil, Loys. Henri Leys, Henri de Braekeleer, James Ensor, Paris, 1925. (Le Peintre-graveur illustré <XIXe et XXe siècles> t. 19)
Lists 132 works

10 Garvens-Garvensburg, Herbert von. James Ensor, Maler, Radierer, Komponist: ein Hinweis mit dem volständigen Katalog seines radierten Werkes als Anhang, Hannover, Ludwig Ey, 1913, 33p. plus 27 plates
Lists 129 works

BOOKS AND ARTICLES

11 Les Arts Plastiques, Brussels, 4no 1:1-61 Ja-F 1950, illus.
Special number devoted to Ensor. Tributes by Paul Fierens, René Huyghe, Jean Cassou, Paul Haesaerts, Louis Lebeer, Jean Stevo. Includes an unpublished letter by Ensor

12 Avermaete, Roger. James Ensor, der Graphiker. Der Cicerone, Berlin, 20hft22:723-9 N 1928, illus.

13 ———James Ensor, Anvers, De Sikkel, 1947, 15p. plus 25 plates (1 col.), port. (Monographies de l'art belge, ser. 1, no. 4)

14 Benson, E. M. James Ensor. Parnassus, New York, 6:1-3 F 1934, illus.

15 Bernard, Charles. James Ensor, Anvers, Édition de "La Revue d'Art," 1929, 15p. plus 21 plates (1 col.). (Études d'art contemporain)
Includes speech given by Ensor at banquet, Feb. 10, 1929

16 Brunt, Aty. James Ensor. Art Flamand et Hollandais, Antwerp, 8e année, 15:155-65 1911, illus.

17 Cahiers de Belgique, Brussels, no 1:1-38 F 1929, illus. (incl. ports.)
Special number devoted to Ensor. Articles by Paul Fierens, A. H. Cornette, J.-E. Sonderegger, and excerpts from critical reviews.

18 Carter, Frederick. James Ensor. Artwork, London, 7no 26:98-108 Summer 1931, illus.

†19 Colin, Paul. James Ensor, Potsdam, Kiepenheuer, 1921, 74 plates

20 ———James Ensor, Berlin, Klinkhardt & Biermann, 1931, 15p. plus 33 plates (1 col.). (Junge Kunst, bd. 59)

21 ———L'impressionisme en Belgique. *In* René Huyghe. Histoire de l'art contemporain: la peinture, Paris, Alcan, 1935, p. 375-81, illus.
Includes biographical and bibliographical notes

22 Coquiot, Gustave. Cubistes, futuristes, passéistes, Paris, Ollendorff, 1914, p. 41-56, illus.

23 Croquez, Albert. La jeunesse de James Ensor. Amour de l'Art, Paris, 27:225-7 1947, illus. (incl. ports.)

24 Cuypers, Firmin. James Ensor, l'homme et l'oeuvre, Paris, Les Écrivains Réunis, 1925, 22p. plus 25 plates

25 ———Aspects et propos de James Ensor, Bruges, Stainforth, 1946, 101p., illus. (incl. facsims.)

26 Delen, Ary. James Ensor. Elsevier's Geïllustreerd Maandschrift, Amsterdam, 21:161-76 1911, illus.

27 Demolder, Eugène. James Ensor. Société Nouvelle, Brussels, 7e année, 2:581-91 1891

†28 ———James Ensor, Bruxelles, P. Lacomblez, 1892

29 Desmeth, Paul. James Ensor, Bruxelles, L. J. Kryn, 1926, 26p. plus 20 plates. (Artistes de Belgique)

30 Eeckhout, van den. In het Ostende van James Ensor. Elsevier's Geïllustreerd Maandschrift, Amsterdam, 81:28-34 1931

31 Fels, Florent. Propos d'artistes, Paris, La Renaissance du Livre, 1925, p. 47-60, illus.

32 ———James Ensor, Genève-Bruxelles, Pierre Cailler, 1947, 64p. plus 68 plates (some col.)
Includes bibliography

33 Fierens, Paul. James Ensor, Paris, G. Crès, 1929, 14p. plus 32 plates. (Les Artistes nouveaux)

34 ———James Ensor, Paris, Hyperion, 1943, 160p. incl. 158 plates (some col.)
Includes bibliography

35 ———Les dessins d'Ensor, Bruxelles, Editions Apollo, 1944, 43p., illus. plus 48 plates

36 La Flandre Littéraire, Ostende, 2no6:334-56 Ja 1924
Special number devoted to Ensor. Articles by Edmond Joly, Claude Bernières, André de Ridder, Gaston Heux and others

37 Fraenger, Wilhelm. James Ensor: *Die Kathedrale.* Die Graphischen Künste, Vienna, 49:81-98 1926, illus.
On etchings by Ensor

38 Haesaerts, Luc & Paul. Flandre: essai sur l'art flamand depuis 1880: l'impressionisme, Paris, Éditions des Chroniques du Jour, 1931, p. 104-279, illus.

39 Hausenstein, Wilhelm. Ensor. Das Kunstblatt, Weimar, 1:11-23 Ja 1918, illus.

40 Hellens, Frans. Un grand peintre belge: Ensor. Art Vivant, Paris, 2:41-4 Ja 15 1926, illus.

41 Hennus, M. F. De etsen van James Ensor. Maandblad voor Beeldende Kunsten, Amsterdam, 4:293-303 1927, illus.

42 History of Modern Painting: Matisse, Munch, Rouault, Fauvism, Expressionism, Geneva, Albert Skira, 1950, p. 101-3, 134-5, col. illus.
Includes biographical and bibliographical notes

43 Jaloux, Edmond. James Ensor. Amour de l'Art, Paris, 7:153-8 1926, illus.

44 Jedlicka, Gotthard. Begegnungen, Basel, Benno Schwabe, 1933, p. 214-49, port.
Also published in 2d ed., Erlenbach-Zürich, Eugen Rentsch, 1945, p. 158-84. Includes statements by Ensor

45 ———James Ensor. Werk, Zurich, 31hft5:133-7 My 1944, illus.

†46 Kobliha, Frantisek. Graficke dilo Jamesa Ensora. Hollar, Prague, 5:27-35 1928

47 Krestovsky, Lydie. La laideur dans l'art à travers les ages, Paris, Éditions du Seuil, 1947, p. 214-24

48 LeRoy, Grégoire. James Ensor, Bruxelles et Paris, Van Oest, 1922, 203p., illus. plus 78 plates

49 Marlier, Georges. James Ensor et le double aspect de son art. Amour de l'Art, Paris, 9:410-18 1928, illus.

50 Maus, Madeleine Octave. Trente années de lutte pour l'art, 1884-1914, Bruxelles, Librairie de l'Oiseau Bleu, 1926, passim

51 Michel, Wilhelm. Das Teuflische und Groteske in der Kunst, München, Piper, 1917, passim, illus.

52 Payro, Julio E. James Ensor, Buenos Aires, Poseidon, 1943, 27p., illus. plus 41 plates. (Biblioteca argentina d'arte)

53 La Plume, Paris, 10no228-32 1898, illus.
Includes articles and comments by Camille Lemonnier, Edmond Picard, Camille Mauclair, Emil Verhaeren, Max Elscamp, Blanche Rousseau, Octave Maus, Maurice des Ombiaux, Maurice Maeterlinck, Pol de Mont, and others. Issued also as single volume under title: James Ensor, peintre et graveur, Paris, Librairie de la Société anonyme "La Plume," 1899, 96p., illus.

54 Podestà, Attilio. James Ensor. Emporium, Bergamo, 111 no661:2-14 Ja 1950, illus.

55 Puyvelde, Leo van. L'ardente peinture d'Ensor, Paris, Gazette des Beaux-Arts et Beaux-Arts, 1939, 46p. plus 29 plates, port.

56 Ridder, André de. James Ensor à Ostende. Variétés, Brussels, 1no2:59-68 Je 15 1928, illus.

57 ———James Ensor, Paris, Ridder, 1930, 64p. plus 60 plates. (Maîtres de l'art moderne)

58 Schwob, Lucien. Ensor, Bruxelles, Impr. van Doorslaer, 1936, 56p., illus. plus 50 plates.
Includes facsimiles of writings by Ensor and statements by the artist

59 Tannenbaum, Libby. James Ensor: prophet of modern fantastic art. Magazine of Art, Washington, D.C., 36:244-9 N 1943, illus.

60 Tugendhold, Y. James Ensor. Apollon, Petrograd, no 1: 24-32 1915, illus.

61 Verhaeren, Emile. James Ensor, Bruxelles, Van Oest, 1908, 132p., illus. plus 35 plates. (Collection des artistes belges contemporains)

62 Woestyne, Karel van de. James Ensor. Elsevier's Geïllustreerd Maandschrift, Amsterdam, 75:73-89 1928, illus.

IMPORTANT EXHIBITIONS: CATALOGUES AND COMMENTARY

1898. Paris. La Plume
For publication issued in connection with exhibition, see bibl. 53

1920. Brussels. Galerie Georges Giroux
Catalogue by J. F. Elslander

1921. Antwerp. L'Art Contemporain
Reviewed in Amour de l'Art, Paris, 2no7:220-1 Jy 1921

1926. Paris. Galerie Barbazanges
Catalogue listing 60 works with introduction by Waldemar George

1927. Hanover. Kestner-Gesellschaft
† Catalogue with articles by Alexander Dörner, Herbert von Garvens-Garvensburg, Wilhelm Fraenger. Exhibition reviewed in Deutsche Kunst und Dekoration, Darmstadt, 60: 151-8 1927

1929. Brussels. Palais des Beaux Arts
Catalogue listing 325 works with preface by François Fosca. Exhibition reviewed in Gand Artistique, 8:44-51 1929; Cahiers de Belgique, Brussels, 2:113-18 1929; Amour de l'Art, Paris, 9:108-9 F 1929

1932. Paris. Musée National du Jeu de Paume
Catalogue listing 179 works with introduction by A. H. Cornette. Exhibition reviewed in Amour de l'Art, Paris, 13:244, 245, 255 Jy-Ag 1932; Renaissance, Paris, 15:153-6 1932; Art Vivant, Paris, no162:348-9 Jy 1932; by André Lhote in his Écrits sur la peinture, Paris, Lumière, 1946, p. 165-9

1936. London. Leicester Galleries
Catalogue listing 95 works with foreword by R. H. Wilenski. Exhibition reviewed in The Listener, London, 16no390:18-19 Jy 1, 1936

1939. Paris. Gazette des Beaux-Arts et Beaux Arts
Catalogue by Leo van Puyvelde listing 211 works. Exhibition reviewed in Beaux Arts, Paris, 76no338:1 Je 23 1939; Studio, London, 118:128-9 1939

1943. Chicago. Art Institute of Chicago
First comprehensive print exhibition in U.S. Article occasioned by exhibition in Gazette des Beaux Arts, New York, 24no922:363-74 D 1943

1944. New York. Buchholz Gallery, Curt Valentin
Catalogue listing 35 works. Introduction by Leo van Puyvelde. Exhibition reviewed in Art Digest, New York, 18:9 Ja 1 1944; Art News, New York, 42:23 Ja 15 1944

1945. Brussels. Galerie Georges Giroux
Catalogue listing 159 works. Preface by Leo van Puyvelde. Includes list of exhibitions. Exhibition reviewed in Emporium, Bergamo, 103:176-80 Ap 1946

1946. London. National Gallery
Catalogue listing 88 works with introduction by Leo van Puyvelde. Organized by the Arts Council of Great Britain; held under the auspices of the Tate Gallery. Exhibition reviewed in Studio, London, 131no639:185 Je 1946; Burlington Magazine, London, 88:97 Ap 1946

1950. Venice. 25th Biennale
26 works listed. Note by Emile Langui. Exhibition reviewed in Emporium, Bergamo, 112no667:17-22 Jy 1950

1951. Antwerp. Musée Royal des Beaux-Arts
Catalogue listing 429 works. Introduction by Walther Vanbeselaere. Includes list of exhibitions

CATALOGUE OF THE EXHIBITION

LENDERS

Mlle Julienne Boogaerts, Brussels; M. Borgers, Ostend, Belgium; Thomas Braun, Brussels; Baron de Broqueville, Brussels; Mme Albert Croquez, Paris; Mme Richard Daveluy, Ostend, Belgium; Philippe Dotremont, Brussels; Mme Charles Franck, Antwerp; Colonel Louis Franck, C.B.E., London; Baron Robert Gendebien, Brussels; Miss Adelaide Milton de Groot, New York; J. Janssen, Antwerp; Mme Henri Jooris, Lille, France; Cléomire Jussiant, Antwerp; Baroness Lambert, Brussels; Roland Leten, Ghent, Belgium; Marcel Mabille, Brussels; Max Motte, Brussels; Mr. and Mrs. Harry J. Rudick, New York; August Tavernier, Ghent, Belgium; Curt Valentin, New York; D. G. Van Beuningen, Vierhouten, Gelderland, The Netherlands; Gustave Van Geluwe, Brussels; Mme Van Weyenbergh, Quaregnon, Belgium.

Cabinet des Estampes, Brussels; Casino Communal, Knokke-le-Zoute, Belgium; Detroit Institute of Arts, Detroit, Mich.; Musée Charlier, Brussels; Musée des Beaux-Arts, Ghent, Belgium; Musée des Beaux-Arts, Liège, Belgium; Musée des Beaux-Arts, Tournai, Belgium; Musée National d'Art Moderne, Paris; Musée Royal des Beaux-Arts, Antwerp; Musées Royaux des Beaux-Arts, Brussels; Museum of Modern Art, New York; Ostend Museum of Art, Ostend, Belgium; Buchholz Gallery, New York.

CATALOGUE

An asterisk (*) preceding the catalogue number indicates that the picture is illustrated. In listing the dimensions, height precedes width.

PAINTINGS

* 1 *Dunes.* 1876. Oil on cardboard, 7 x 9". Lent by Mlle Julienne Boogaerts, Brussels. *Ill. p. 28*

* 2 *Estaminet.* 1876 or 1877. Oil on cardboard, 7½ x 9¼". Lent by Gustave Van Geluwe, Brussels. *Ill. p. 28*

3 *Beach.* 1877. Oil on cardboard, 7 x 8½". Lent by Gustave Van Geluwe, Brussels

* 4 *Self Portrait.* 1879. Oil on panel, 7⅞ x 5¾". Lent by Marcel Mabille, Brussels. *Ill. p. 31*

5 *Self Portrait.* 1879. Oil sketch (for no. 4, above), on panel, 6¾ x 5⅛". Lent by Marcel Mabille, Brussels

* 6 *Girl With the Turned-Up Nose.* 1879. Oil on canvas, 21¼ x 17¾". Lent by Royal Museum of Fine Arts, Antwerp. *Ill. p. 30*

* 7 *The Lamp Boy.* 1880. Oil on canvas, 59¾ x 35¾". Lent by Royal Museum of Fine Arts, Brussels. *Ill. p. 33*

* 8 *Still Life.* 1880. Oil on canvas, 31½ x 39¼". Lent by Museum of Fine Arts, Tournai, Belgium. *Ill. p. 34*

* 9 *Lady with a Fan.* 1880. Oil on canvas, 52⅛ x 33". Lent by J. Janssen, Antwerp. *Ill. p. 36*

*10 *The Bourgeois Salon.* 1880. Oil sketch (for no. 11, below), on canvas, 25⅝ x 22½". Lent by Gustave Van Geluwe, Brussels. *Ill. p. 38*

*11 *The Bourgeois Salon.* 1881. Oil on canvas, 51⅛ x 43¼". Lent by Mme Henri Jooris, Lille, France. *Ill. p. 39*

*12 *Boulevard Van Iseghem at Ostend.* 1881. Oil on panel, 13 x 10¼″. Lent by Mlle Julienne Boogaerts, Brussels. *Ill. p. 35*

*13 *Somber Lady.* 1881. Oil on canvas, 39¼ x 31⅞″. Lent by Royal Museum of Fine Arts, Brussels. *Ill. p. 45*

14 *Lady in Blue.* 1881. Oil on canvas, 26¾ x 23″. Lent by Royal Museum of Fine Arts, Brussels

15 *Fans and Fabrics.* 1881. Oil on canvas, 19 x 21″. Lent by Mlle Julienne Boogaerts, Brussels

16 *Pears.* 1881. Oil on canvas, 15¾ x 19¾″. Lent by Philippe Dotremont, Brussels

17 *Still Life.* 1882. Oil on canvas, 30¾ x 38½″. Lent by Museum of Fine Arts, Liège, Belgium

18 *The Painter Willy Finch.* 1882. Oil on canvas, 43¼ x 37½″. Lent by J. Janssen, Antwerp

19 *Troubled (La Dame en détresse).* 1882. Oil on canvas, 39½ x 31½″. Lent by Musée National d'Art Moderne, Paris

*20 *Portrait of the Painter in a Flowered Hat.* 1883. Oil on canvas, 29½ x 25⅝″. Lent by Mlle Julienne Boogaerts, Brussels. *Ill. p. 43*

*21 *Scandalized Masks.* 1883. Oil on canvas, 53 x 44″. Lent by Royal Museum of Fine Arts, Brussels. *Ill. in color p. 13*

22 *Ostend Rooftops.* 1884. Oil on canvas, 43¼ x 52¾″. Lent by Colonel Louis Franck, C.B.E., London

23 *Hotel de Ville, Brussels.* 1885. Oil on canvas, 39¼ x 30″. Lent by Museum of Fine Arts, Liège, Belgium

24 *Children Dressing.* 1886. Oil on canvas, 53 x 39½″. Lent by Cléomire Jussiant, Antwerp

*25 *Carnival on the Beach.* 1887. Oil on canvas, 22 x 28″. Lent by Mme Van Weyenbergh, Quaregnon, Belgium. *Ill. in color p. 15*

*26 *The Tribulations of Saint Anthony.* 1887. Oil on canvas, 46⅜ x 66″. Collection The Museum of Modern Art, New York. *Ill. p. 66*

*27 *Entry of Christ into Brussels in 1889.* 1888. Oil on canvas, 8′5½″ x 14′1½″. Lent by Casino Communal, Knokke-le-Zoute, Belgium. *Ill. p. 70, details: 69, 72, 73, and color frontispiece*

*28 *Masks Confronting Death.* 1888. Oil on canvas, 31½ x 39¼″. Lent by Gustave Van Geluwe, Brussels. *Ill. p. 80*

29 *Garden of Love.* 1888. Oil on canvas, 38½ x 44″. Lent by Cléomire Jussiant, Antwerp

30 *Christ in Agony.* 1888 (?). Oil on panel, 6¼ x 8¼″. Lent by Marcel Mabille, Brussels

31 *Fall of the Rebellious Angels.* 1889 or 1888. Oil on canvas, 43¼ x 52¾″. Lent by Royal Museum of Fine Arts, Antwerp

*32 *Astonishment of the Mask Wouse.* 1889. Oil on canvas, 42⅞ x 52″. Lent by Royal Museum of Fine Arts, Antwerp. *Ill. p. 82*

*33 *Skeletons Trying to Warm Themselves.* 1889. Oil on canvas, 29½ x 23⅝″. Lent by Baron Robert Gendebien, Brussels. *Ill. p. 79*

*34 *Old Woman with Masks.* 1889. Oil on canvas, 21⅝ x 18″. Lent by Roland Leten, Ghent, Belgium. *Ill. p. 81*

*35 *Attributes of the Studio.* 1889. Oil on canvas, 32½ x 44½″. Lent by Roland Leten, Ghent, Belgium. *Ill. in color p. 17*

36 *Still Life with Fruits.* 1889. Oil on canvas, 22¾ x 29½″. Lent by Baroness Lambert, Brussels

37 *Flowers and Butterflies.* 1889. Oil on canvas, 23½ x 19¾″. Lent by Musée Charlier, Brussels

*38 *Boats.* 1890. Oil on canvas, 24⅜ x 26¾″. Lent by Royal Museum of Fine Arts, Antwerp. *Ill. p. 93*

*39 *Forbidding Figure (Portrait of the Artist's Aunt).* 1890. Oil on panel, 9⅝ x 7½″. Lent by Marcel Mabille, Brussels. *Ill. p. 86*

*40 *Murder.* 1890. Oil on canvas, 23⅝ x 30″. Lent by Marcel Mabille, Brussels. *Ill. p. 85*

*41 *The Domain of Arnheim* (cf. story by Edgar Allan Poe). 1890. Oil on canvas, 31½ x 39¼″. Lent by Thomas Braun, Brussels. *Ill. p. 87*

42 *Still Life with Peaches.* 1890. Oil on panel, 7½ x 9½″. Lent by Marcel Mabille, Brussels

43 *Man of Sorrows.* 1891. Oil on panel, 8¼ x 6¼″. Lent by Roland Leten, Ghent, Belgium

44 *Christ Calming the Waters.* 1891. Oil on canvas, 31¼ x 39½″. Lent by Gustave Van Geluwe, Brussels

*45 *Skeletons Fighting for the Body of a Hanged Man.* 1891. Oil on canvas, 23¼ x 29⅛″. Lent by Royal Museum of Fine Arts, Antwerp. *Ill. in color p. 19*

46 *Grotesque Singers.* 1891. Oil on canvas, 6¼ x 8½″. Lent by Marcel Mabille, Brussels

*47 *Music, Rue de Flandre.* 1891. Oil on panel, 9½ x 7½″. Lent by Royal Museum of Fine Arts, Antwerp. *Ill. p. 94*

48 *The Gendarmes.* 1892. Oil on canvas, 19¾ x 25½″. Lent by Ostend Museum of Art, Ostend, Belgium

49 *Consoling Virgin.* 1892. Oil on panel, 15¾ x 15″. Lent by August Tavernier, Ghent, Belgium

50 *Melancholy Fishwives.* 1892. Oil on canvas, 39¼ x 31½″. Lent by Max Motte, Brussels

51 *The Cabbage.* 1892. Oil on canvas, 32 x 39½″. Lent by Philippe Dotremont, Brussels

*52 *The Skate.* 1892. Oil on canvas, 31½ x 39¼″. Lent by Royal Museum of Fine Arts, Brussels. *Ill. in color p. 23*

*53 *Shells.* 1895. Oil on canvas, 39½ x 32″. Lent by Baron de Broqueville, Brussels. *Ill. p. 91*

*54 *Portrait of the Artist Surrounded by Masks.* 1899. Oil on canvas, 47¼ x 31½″. Lent by Cléomire Jussiant, Antwerp. *Ill. p. 105*

55 *Boats on the Beach.* 1900. Oil on canvas, 23½ x 29½″. Lent by Gustave Van Geluwe, Brussels

*56 *Double Portrait* (The Artist and Mlle Augusta Boogaerts). 1905. Oil on panel, 15½ x 13″. Lent by Mlle Julienne Boogaerts, Brussels. *Ill. p. 108*

*57 *The Game of Love* (Setting for the 2nd Act of the artist's ballet). 1914. Oil on canvas, 66⅛ x 81⅛″. Lent by J. Janssen, Antwerp. *Ill. p. 110, detail, p. 111*

*57a *The Artist's Mother in Death.* 1915. Oil. Lent by Mme Richard Daveluy, Ostend, Belgium. *Ill. p. 114*

*58 *Droll Smokers.* c. 1920. Oil on canvas, 29½ x 25¼". Lent by Mlle Julienne Boogaerts, Brussels. *Ill. p. 116*

59 *Fairy Ballet.* Oil on canvas, 20 x 24". Lent by Detroit Institute of Arts

*60 *Banquet of the Starved.* c. 1925. Oil on canvas, 45⅛ x 57⅜". Lent by Miss Adelaide Milton de Groot, New York. *Ill. p. 117*

*61 *The Studio of the Artist.* c. 1930. Oil on canvas, 33 x 26". Lent by D. G. Van Beuningen, Vierhouten, Gelderland, The Netherlands. *Ill. p. 120*

*62 *My Austere Visage Lighted by Moons.* 1937. Oil on panel, 13¼ x 10". Lent by Mr. and Mrs. Harry J. Rudick, New York. *Ill. p. 119*

The Artist's Sister. c.1883. Pencil sketch, 8¾ x 6¾". Collection Mlle Julienne Boogaerts, Brussels

DRAWINGS AND WATERCOLORS

A group of five drawings lent by the Royal Museum of Fine Arts, Antwerp:

63 *Fiacre and Horses.* 1881. Sketch, 8⅝ x 7"

64 *Story without Words.* 1881. Sketch, 8¾ x 7"

65 *Scaffold.* Sketch, 8⅞ x 3⅛"

66 *Frottage.* 5⅞ x 5"

67 *Frottage.* With watercolor, 2½ x 8¼"

*68 *Christ in Agony.* 1888. Black chalk and charcoal, 23⅜ x 29⅛". Lent by Royal Museum of Fine Arts, Brussels. *Ill. p. 58*

69 *Battle of the Golden Spurs.* 1891. Colored pencil and ink on panel, 14¾ x 18". Lent by Royal Museum of Fine Arts, Brussels

*70 *Figures.* 1880. Watercolor, 9⅝ x 13". Lent by Museum of Fine Arts, Ghent, Belgium. *Ill. p. 51*

A group of 26 drawings lent by Mlle Julienne Boogaerts, Brussels. Nos. 72-87 are small sketches, mostly done in notebooks in the early 1880's.

*71 *Young Sailor.* 1880. Charcoal on paper, 28¾ x 23¼". *Ill. p. 32*

72 *Parasol.* Pencil, 8⅝ x 6⅝"

73 Sketch (Hat and leg of a man). Pencil, 8⅝ x 6⅝"

74 *Lamps.* Pencil

75 *Fiacre and Figures.* Watercolor

76 *Street with a Horseman.* Pencil sketch

77 *Street* (Three horses with figures). Pencil sketch, 8⅞ x 13¾"

*78 Pencil sketch (White horse and figures). c. 1883. 6¾ x 8¾". *Ill. p. 50*

79 *Horse and Dog.* Pencil sketch, 6 x 6⅝"

80 *Figures.* Pencil sketch, 6⅝ x 8⅝"

81 Pencil sketch (Hands and profile). 8⅝ x 6⅝"

82 *The Artist's Sister Asleep.* Pencil sketch, 8¾ x 6¼"

*83 *The Artist's Sister Asleep* (Small figures). Pencil sketch, 8⅝ x 6⅝". *Ill. at left*

84 *Sleeping Figure* (The Aunt or Grandmother). Pencil sketch

85 Sketch (Mme Ensor and figures). 9 x 13¾"

86 Sketch (Mme Ensor and a profile head). Pencil, 8⅝ x 6⅝"

*87 *Sleep.* c. 1883. Pencil sketch, 8¾ x 6¼". *Ill. p. 48*

*88 *Self Portrait* (Mon portrait triste et somptueux). 1886. Pencil, 8¾ x 6¼". *Ill. p. 54*

89 Sketch for the 1888 etching *The Terrible Sentinel.* Pencil, 9 x 13¾"

90 *Sloth* (La Paresse). Pencil, 9 x 13¾"

91 *Boulevard Van Iseghem, Ostend.* 1889. Pencil on panel, 8⅝ x 6⅝"

92 *Fiacre, Ostend Casino.* Crayon, 5½ x 9"

*93 *Calvary.* Pencil and color on panel, 6¾ x 8¾". *Ill. p. 58*

*94 *Christ in Hell.* 1891. Pencil, 8¾ x 11¾". *Ill. p. 96*

*95 *Small Persian Torture.* Colored drawing, 8¼ x 9½". *Ill. p. 96*

96 *"My Hand in 1928."* Colored drawing, 8⅝ x 12¼"

97 *Grimacet, Graco-Cigaret, Gargouillis, Cafrousse, Panachet, Sansonnet, Smoufel* (figures from the ballet *The Game of Love*). 1912. Drawing, 10½ x 13⅜". Lent by M. Borgers, Ostend, Belgium

98 *Figures.* 1880. Watercolor, 9¼ x 12¾". Lent by Mme Albert Croquez, Paris

99 *Romans of the Decadence.* 1890. Colored drawing, 7½ x 11". Lent by Mme Albert Croquez, Paris

100 *Self Portrait with "The Entry of Christ into Brussels."* c. 1930. Pastel, 22¾ x 17". Lent by Mme Albert Croquez, Paris

The following six drawings from the collection of Marcel Mabille, Brussels:

*101 *The Dead Christ Watched Over by Angels.* 1886. Drawing, 6¼ x 8½". *Ill. p. 59*

102 *Skeleton Musician.* 1888. Drawing, 8¼ x 6¼"

103 *Battle of Waterloo.* 1891. Colored drawing, 8⅞ x 24⅝"

104 *The Rout of the Mercenaries.* 1892. Drawing, 6¼ x 8½"

105 *Mlle Demolder as a Toreador.* 1895. Watercolor, 10½ x 13⅜"

*106 *Skeletons Playing Billiards.* 1903. Drawing, 9½ x 11¾". *Ill. p. 106*

107 *Banquet.* Pencil, 4⅞ x 7". Lent by Buchholz Gallery, New York

*108 Notebook. 1929 ff. 7⅛ x 8⅜". Lent by Curt Valentin, New York. *Page ill. p. 118*

*109 Notebook page. 1883. Pencil, 8¾ x 6⅞". Private collection, Brooklyn, New York. *Ill. p. 53*

110 Notebook page. Pencil, 8¾ x 6⅞". Private collection, Brooklyn, New York

PRINTS

Numbers are from the catalogue of Loys Delteil, bibl. no. 9

*D. 106 *The Scavenger.* 1896. Etching, later hand-colored in watercolor by the artist, 4¾ x 3⅜". Lent by Mlle Julienne Boogaerts, Brussels. *Ill. p. 99*

*D. 121 *Anger* (From The Seven Deadly Sins series). 1904. Etching, later hand-colored in watercolor by the artist, 3⅞ x 5⅞". Lent by Mme Charles Franck, Antwerp. *Ill. p. 106*

The following etchings have been lent by the Cabinet des Estampes in Brussels:

D. 1 *Christ Mocked.* 1886. 9½ x 6¼"

*D. 6 *Iston, Pouffamatus, Cracozie, and Transmouff, Celebrated Persian Physicians, Examining the Stools of King Darius after the Battle of Arbela.* 1886. 9⅝ x 7¼". *Ill. p. 62*

*D. 7 *The Cathedral* (First of two plates of this subject). 1886. 9½ x 7½". *Ill. p. 60*

*D. 10 *Devil's Sabbath.* 1887. 8⅝ x 10½". *Ill. p. 63*

*D. 23 *Combat of Demons.* 1888. 10⅜ x 12⅛". *Ill. p. 75*

*D. 34 *My Portrait in 1960.* 1888. 2¾ x 4¾". *Ill. p. 61*

*D. 36 *The Terrible Sentinel.* 1888. 7 x 9⅜". *Ill. p. 76*

D. 37 *Cataclysm.* 1888. 7 x 9⅜"

D. 44 *Boats.* 1888. 7 x 9⅜"

D. 49 *Boats on the Beach.* 1888. 7 x 9⅜"

D. 78 *Roman Triumph.* 1889. 7 x 9½"

*D. 86 *The Judges.* 1894. 7⅛ x 9⅜". *Ill. p. 101*

D. 88 *The Devils Dzitts and Hihanox Conducting Christ into Hell.* 1895. 5½ x 7"

*D. 91 *Demons Tormenting Me.* 1895. 4⅝ x 6⅛". *Ill. p. 103*

D. 93 *Gamblers.* 1895. 7 x 9½"

*D. 95 *The Battle of the Golden Spurs.* 1895. 7 x 9½". *Ill. p. 97*

*D. 104 *Death Pursuing the People.* 1896. 9⅜ x 7¼". *Ill. p. 98*

*D. 112 *The Vengeance of Hop Frog.* (cf. story by Edgar Allan Poe). 1898. 14⅜ x 9¾". *Ill. p. 65*

*D. 114 *The Entry of Christ into Brussels.* 1898. 9¾ x 14". *Ill. p. 74*

D. 115 *Beach at Ostend.* 1899. 8⅞ x 11"

D. 127 *Peste dessous, peste dessus, peste partout.* 1904. 7⅝ x 11¾"

D. 129 *Beach at La Panne.* 1904. 4 x 5⅞"

This book has been printed in August, 1951, for the Trustees of The Museum of Modern Art, New York by Frederick W. Schmidt, Inc., New York, who did the color section, and Case, Lockwood & Brainard, Hartford, Connecticut. The color engravings were made by Etablissements Jean Malvaux, Brussels. Jacket design by Jack Dunbar